YOU AND YOUR PARTNER, INC.

YOU AND YOUR PARTNER, INC.

Entrepreneurial Couples
Succeeding in Business, Life & Love

MIRIAM HAWLEY & JEFFREY MCINTYRE

Miriam Hawley

& Jeffrey McIntyre

ENLIGNMENT PRESS

2012

Enlignment Press

1770 Massachusetts Avenue #132,
Cambridge, Massachusetts 02140-2808.

www.enlignment.com

~.~

Library of Congress Cataloguing-in-Publication Data
Hawley, Miriam and McIntyre, Jeffrey
You and Your Partner, Inc.
Entrepreneurial Couples Succeeding in Business, Life and Love

ISBN 978-0-615-64897-2
1. Relationships, Marriage and Family 2. Business 3. Motivation and Self-development
4. Entrepreneurs and Entrepreneurship

Edited by Paul Bennett and Mary Elizabeth Wheeler
Master Edit by Judy Katz, ghostbooksters.com
Art Direction by Wendy Glavin
Book design by Rebecca Saraceno, RebeccaInk
Cover design: © OlimpiaZagnoli / marlenaagency.com
Printing by BYJ Communications, Inc.

TABLE OF CONTENTS

ACKNOWLEDGMENTS

J EFFREY AND MIRIAM WOULD LIKE to dedicate this book
to the brave couples throughout the world who have formed
business partnerships to create deeper meaning in their lives and,
ultimately, for the multitudes of others that they touch.
We ourselves have been so heartened by our respective parents and
role models, Ada and Bob McIntyre and Helane and Abe Press, with their
eternal love and leadership. We are proud to see these principles in action
as our children and our grandchildren continue to amaze us with their
choices and endeavors.

Earlier in the writing process, we were extremely fortunate to have the
honesty and encouragement of reviewers and editors such as Lauren and
Bob Bellon, Lisa Dennis, Heidi Sparkes Guber, George Klavens, Ken
Lizotte and Kate M. Victory. We are also thankful to Paul B. Brown for
his invaluable advice and direction.

The writing, editing and organizing skills of editors Paul Bennett and
Mary Elizabeth Wheeler truly made the project a reality; they are irre-
placeable. We, Jeffrey and Miriam, a team of two, soon became a group
of four as we forged ahead together. We are deeply grateful for Paul and
Mary Elizabeth's wisdom, intelligence, persistence and friendship. We
thank them from the bottom of our hearts.

We thought we were nearing our conclusion when Judy Katz, writer
and editor extraordinaire, came on the scene. Her vision, dedication, creativity and humor brought You and Your Partner, Inc., over the finish line.
We are forever grateful to her.

Out of the hundreds of couples interviews we conducted, the final
50 respondents' candor about the challenges and successes they faced
were uniquely rich, creative and diverse experiences. We were moved and
humbled by each and every couple who participated so generously, and
want to thank and honor each of these individual couples. They are:

- ♥ Rosi and Brian Amador
- ♥ Mark Andrus and Stacy Madison
- ♥ Leslie and Ron Arslanian
- ♥ Liza Roeser Atwood and Blu Atwood
- ♥ Rich and Antra Borofsky
- ♥ Peggy Burns and Richard Tubman
- ♥ Ginger Burr and Marion Davis
- ♥ Katharine and Alan Cahn
- ♥ Wendy Capland and Chris Michaud
- ♥ Philip Cass and Laura Weisel
- ♥ Alina and Ron Chand
- ♥ Jennifer Christian and David Siktberg
- ♥ Jeffrey and Sandy Davis
- ♥ Allen and Theresa Daytner
- ♥ Ian Dowe and Allison Reilly
- ♥ Anne and Christopher Ellinger
- ♥ Matthew and Terces Engelhart
- ♥ Claudette and Ade Faison
- ♥ Laurie and Jeffrey Ford
- ♥ Mark and Kate Friedman
- ♥ Barry Friedman and Valerie Gates
- ♥ Suzanne and Dwight Frindt
- ♥ Mary Gillach and Kathy Halley
- ♥ Sandy and Lon Golnick
- ♥ Peter Hansen and Petra Krauledat
- ♥ Peter Kevorkian and Patti Giuliano
- ♥ Gina LaRoche and Alan Price
- ♥ Jean and Howard Le Vaux
- ♥ Katy and Philip Leakey

- ♥ Jessica Lipnack and Jeffrey Stamps (1945–2012)
- ♥ Nick and Mitra Lore
- ♥ Rebecca Marston and Alexander Voss
- ♥ Sherri and Terry McArdle
- ♥ David Nicholas and David Miranowicz
- ♥ Marguerite Piret and Richard Rosen
- ♥ Scott and Sue Richardson
- ♥ Judy Rosenberg and Eliot Winograd
- ♥ Steven and Marjorie Sayer
- ♥ Linda and Mel Shapiro
- ♥ Ellyn Spragins and John Witty
- ♥ Dorothy and Wayne Stingley
- ♥ Lynne and Bill Twist
- ♥ Wynn and Douglas Waggoner
- ♥ Joyce and Jack Zimmerman

We also want to recognize all of our communities and teachers that played a part in the evolution of the book:

- Our Bodies, Ourselves: Miriam's experience as one of the founders of the Boston Women's Health Book Collective provided a model for collaborative writing. Writing in partnership as a practice had succeeded in the past, so why not now?!
- The community at Mountain View Lake, New Hampshire
- The Pachamama Alliance community of founders and facilitators
- The Sufficiency Communities: The Global Sufficiency Network, The Sufficiency Foundation, The Source Mamas and groups committed to the sufficiency conversation
- The community of Landmark Education seminar leaders and participants
- Shambhala Buddhist Community and the Buddhist Recovery Network
- Our partners in Systems Perspectives LLC

- The Action Trumps Everything community (originally Entrepreneurial Thought in Action and now Just Start)
- Our original families — Miriam's mother, our siblings, our children, their partners, our grandchildren — and our chosen family of friends and their children

All of the above have been teachers, as have our Buddhist teachers and teachers of mystical Judaism.

Two other most noteworthy people are Simon and Glorianne Wittes, who were our couples' therapists. They married us a long time ago. We have always marveled at their extraordinary loving relationship and business partnership. Their insights and guidance continue to inspire and sustain us. We honor them.

"The whole is greater than the sum of its parts."

—ARISTOTLE (384 BC–322 BC)
GREEK PHILOSOPHER; STUDENT OF PLATO;
TUTOR TO ALEXANDER THE GREAT

COPRENEURSHIP: AN EXCITING AND DYNAMIC MODEL FOR THE 21ST CENTURY

O VER THE COURSE OF OUR 30-year marriage, which included various careers for each of us, we were always in search of a more harmonious life, so we joined forces and created a business together. The work we do today, as executive coaches and leadership consultants, grew out of our previous experience and naturally led us into coaching business couples.

We are now happier than ever. But something was still missing. We wanted to find like-minded people to connect with. So began a new two-year journey of interviewing hundreds of couples who had likewise created businesses together. Through this process we came to realize that we were part of what is now a fast-growing trend.

This was such an amazing and enlightening experience that we decided to share our findings in the hope of providing a unique life choice for others in search of balance, harmony, freedom and prosperity through working together. It was hard to eliminate anyone but eventually we did. We chose the 50 most representative and relatable couples, all of whom had candidly shared their fascinating life stories.

The couples you will meet are diverse in age, background, location, size of business, type of business or industry. In these challenging economic times, these couples have discovered unique solutions for managing their careers, families and relationships. This choice is, of course, not without its challenges. However, it is a choice that can have a huge payout. Undertaken with sensitivity, intelligence and love, these partnerships offer rich rewards.

What motivated these couples to take on the challenges of being in business together? Some created their businesses as an alternative to "Corporate America" and the stresses of juggling two professional careers. Others inherited family businesses and wanted to honor the investments their predecessors had made. Those with an entrepreneurial spirit wanted to see their good ideas come to fruition. Sometimes opportunities presented themselves, and the couple was at the right place at the right time. Some reacted to a layoff or to added travel obligations that interfered with child rearing. Still others, eager to take charge of their own destinies, made this choice to gain the freedom of a whole new lifestyle.

We were deeply moved and inspired by the ways in which the couples we interviewed embodied their values of integrity, courage, excellence and contribution in both their personal and professional lives. They were also committed to communication, collaboration and extending themselves to their communities.

The couples we interviewed do not compromise their values for profit, though of course they are profitable and fully intend to continue to be. Rather, they measure their success by the quality of the products and services they offer. They also employ their values to offer new possibilities and opportunities for themselves, their families, their communities and the world. They likewise honor people as full human beings in every aspect of their business, whether employee, strategic partner, vendor, customer or client.

From this work and the interviews we conducted, we have identified seven key elements that we believe every couple in business needs to regularly build upon. These seven chapters are the heart of this book, and comprise the context for the exploration you are about to undertake.

When your business and relationship are thriving, your ability and opportunities to contribute to the community and the world are also amplified. We hope these stories will inspire you to begin a copreneurship journey or bring your co-executive support of each other to a whole new level.

May you reach for your own dreams and the breakthrough success that lies ahead.

— MIRIAM HAWLEY AND JEFFREY MCINTYRE

YOU AND YOUR PARTNER, INC.

"Act as if what you do makes a difference. It does."

—WILLIAM JAMES (1842–1910)
BRITISH PSYCHOLOGIST AND AUTHOR

CHAPTER ONE

DEFINING THE STRUCTURE AND OBJECTIVES OF YOUR PROFESSIONAL PARTNERSHIP

MAYBE YOU HAVE AN IDEA for a business you think you'd like to start and run with your life partner. It's an idea you've been thinking or dreaming about for a while, and now you are ready to answer your calling. Or perhaps you and your significant other are already in business together and want to take it to a higher level of achievement. Either way, your life is going to change, and we want to prepare you for what lies ahead.

Couples are inspired to enter into business together for a wide variety of reasons, and we have uncovered the four prime motivators that act as driving forces to build and sustain a business partnership over time. You might see your own impetus described here, or recognize several that operate in concert.

Four Main Motivators

1. **The Practical Partnership** — choosing to develop a plan to make money.

2. **The Tradition Behind Your Partnership** — growing up in entrepreneurial families and inheriting a business, a world view or the entrepreneurial spirit.

3. **The Vision for Your Partnership** — envisioning your way of living and working together, embodying particular values.

4. **The Mission for Your Partnership** — creating a mission for your contribution to the world.

Something prompted your specific business partnership, beginning with a leap of faith. We begin by illustrating how these four motivations have manifested themselves in our story.

Through Miriam's Eyes:

In our case, we were mental health professionals long before we saw ourselves as a couple in business. Another common thread for us was our activism and concern for the world at large. Both of us were involved in the civil rights and anti-war movements in the sixties. I went on to play a major role in creating the women's movement and the women's health movement as one of the original founders and co-authors of *Our Bodies, Ourselves.* This was my passion and part-time avocation.

The other part of my career was spent as a social work practitioner. At first, I served as a community organizer in a Boston area settlement house, and then as a clinical social worker at a local hospital. By this time I had two young children and was getting divorced. It was at that hospital, in 1971, that Jeffrey and I met. Even within the boundaries of the medical institution, I was entrepreneurial. I started a group for young children from the ages of four to 12 to discuss their parents' alcoholism. My colleagues said the kids wouldn't talk to me, but eventually they did. I was inspired to assume this role as a new challenge, and Jeffrey was supportive of me. He was also innovative, as the organizer of one of the first non-traditional trainings in the field of family therapy, addictions and family systems thinking. He initiated dedicated community service teams and learned how to conduct successful interventions.

About five years later, weary of dysfunctional organizational dynamics, I began an independent practice. I don't remember how I thought about the financial ramifications of that choice but I did become successful in private practice and especially enjoyed making my own hours, which provided more free time for me to accommodate my children's schedules.

Jeffrey and I married in 1978 while he was establishing his independent practice after having graduated from Antioch University's Graduate School of Professional Psychology. We became a "blended family" — I brought two children, and he brought one large dog. Jeffrey joined me in private practice a few years later, before our son was born. He was eager for us to establish a well-respected psychotherapy and training business. He insisted that we intentionally define and brand our business and conduct yearly and quarterly planning for our future success. Although I resisted, eventually his sage advice made sense and we soon began to enjoy the results of our acting more like a business.

Clearly, the first motivation for us was practical. I left the hospital to have more freedom and control of my work. Since it worked out well on many fronts, I continued along that path.

There were other forces in play as well. Jeffrey and I were many years into our practices when managed care challenged our professional right to practice in the way we had been trained. If we wanted to stay solvent, we, like all mental health professionals, had to confront the business realities of a changing medical delivery system, whether we wanted to or not. So we did.

We also had traditions of entrepreneurship in our families. Both of our grandfathers and one aunt, two uncles and several cousins were successful business owners and entrepreneurs. We watched them take ideas and develop them into companies, creating profitable services and products. These family members also espoused values we likewise aspired to: a sense of freedom, independence and creativity along with productivity and profitability.

In addition to financial freedom, I observed that one aunt and uncle had more power than most people to determine the course of their life. They offered me a window into another way to generate satisfying and profitable work. My parents, for their part, were passionate about being related to other people. Their relationships, more than the work itself, sustained them, even beyond retirement. What I learned from them about the importance of relationships has contributed to our business success.

I was motivated by the tradition of activism I inherited from my parents. I learned that when you see something that is unjust or could be better, you talk with others, gather a community together and help to create an organization to address the problem. In this way my parents contributed greatly to the development of my entrepreneurial spirit. A good example that demonstrates this principle is how I and the Boston Women's Health Collective brought the book *Our Bodies, Ourselves* into being. We changed the global conversation about women's reproductive health and sexuality.

But my aunt and uncle had something that my parents didn't have: a thriving business partnership in addition to their relationship as a couple, and I wanted that too.

Our private practice served us and our family well while our children were growing up. We could work from home and, in between client appointments, chauffeur them to doctors' appointments and play dates, attend soccer games, swim meets and performances. Then one day (too fast!) all three of our children were grown. They had left for college, were living in different cities or traveling the globe, creating their adult lives. At the same time, we had begun to outgrow the therapy business. We knew how to do it well, and it was an honor and a privilege to contribute to our clients' lives. But we began to feel an urge to expand into the world beyond our therapy offices, and explore new work challenges that would stretch us to grow and allow us to make an even greater contribution.

To shape this vision, we reflected on how we could take our relationship skills, which are at the core of what we have to offer, and use them to enhance business relationships and leadership in the greater arena. We realized that we could make a difference anywhere we chose and that we wanted to teach other professionals and business people in executive and leadership positions how to increase their personal effectiveness and satisfaction. We knew how to teach people to listen deeply to themselves, get clear about what they wanted, create a vision, develop and identify their community and their collaborators, and get into action to produce desired results. All of this occurred inside our shared vision, both believing that together we could make a difference in the world by making a difference in the lives of each individual with whom we worked.

We began to envision our new venture, which was called Enlignment, Inc., a coaching, consulting and training firm, specializing in personal fulfillment and transformational leadership. From our past experiences, we were drawn to working with entrepreneurial individuals, couples and families that wanted to cultivate thriving partnerships and businesses. I was particularly attracted to the idea of fostering leadership in women.

Today our vision is to unleash the potential power inherent in every relationship with the underlying mission of generating profitability, generosity, committed action and constant learning. We are passionate advocates for generating collaboration and creativity through partnering with individuals, families and organizations to help them flourish.

Through Jeffrey's Eyes:
I grew up in Rochester, New York, in an "Eastman Kodak" family where founder George Eastman practiced what I would term "welfare capitalism." In other words, he did everything he could to keep the unions at bay by supplying everything his workers needed. One of the best aspects of

employment was a generous vacation policy. Every summer, we went to the Adirondack Mountains.

In addition to some great role modeling of negotiation by my parents, I heard stories of a distant great grandfather, Archibald McIntyre, who owned iron mines. A mountain range in the heart of the Adirondacks was named after him. All those memories lay dormant until I was on a canoeing trip during the summer of 1988 when Miriam and I and our son Noah visited the Adirondack Museum. Greeting us at the entranceway to the mining building was an impressive diorama of the McIntyre mines. Viewing the exhibit opened up a whole world of entrepreneurial life within the McIntyre family that I had not known. Iron mines, steam locomotives and the funding of the Erie Canal were all connected to great grandfather McIntyre. I discovered stories of his life to read to our son. I wished I could have shared my excitement with my father but, sadly, he died in January 1989.

Death often focuses the mind on what's truly important. A powerful consequence in my life was realizing how tired I was, after twenty years, of the endless discussions of hospital bureaucratic policy that did not serve our clients' needs.

By the summer of 1989, I decided to leave the hospital and enter completely into independent psychotherapy practice with Miriam. In the first two years we had some difficult conflicts. We followed the suggestions we often give our clients and located a couple who did excellent couples therapy. We began to do the business planning Miriam was describing earlier. Soon began the expansion of our offerings to couples and families in recovery from various addictions. We became more businesslike in everything we did, and added training to our services. It was a pragmatic choice based on concerns about time and money.

My career choices had always been driven by a sense of mission, including civil rights and social justice work. After college, I created addiction treatment programs for those being treated for mental health issues. I also worked with the Commonwealth of Massachusetts to deinstitutionalize mental health patients. This sense of mission had at its core a conviction that there is more at stake in life than just meeting our own needs. I felt committed to making a difference in the lives of ignored and underserved people. My father's teaching — to engage in something bigger than myself and embody a sense of purpose in everything I do — became a major force in shaping the growth and development of Enlignment, Inc.

So here we are...

This book, and the path that led us here, is an entrepreneurial venture in much the same spirit as our book, *Our Bodies, Ourselves.* We have invested our energy, time and money with the same hope: to make a difference in the world. In this moment of our lives, we especially want to contribute to couples who are considering a business venture together, as well as couples who are currently in business and facing all the known and unknown challenges that this choice presents.

In the next sections of this chapter you will hear the stories of people who have identified their primary motivating force for a business start-up. If you are considering going into business together, you can identify the forces that are motivating you. If you have been in business awhile, you can take the opportunity to reflect again on what forces are driving your partnership. Like us, you may find more than one thread.

Motivating Force 1: The Practical Partnership

Entrepreneurs are very practical people. Whether they begin by having a great business idea or through inheriting someone else's great idea, they succeed by seeking out partners who will complement their skill sets, energy and drive. When that person turns out to be your life partner, it can double the pleasure and fun. It can also open a Pandora's Box of complications.

Although a few of the couples we interviewed began their businesses and intimate partnerships simultaneously, the large majority created their business partnerships by building upon the foundation of an established personal relationship. Many wanted one of them or both to be home-based when their children were young, or until they were ready for the next level business risk and needed a trusted partner. Some were challenging the ways in which their lives had been structured, eager to find better answers for themselves and their nuclear or even extended families.

Seizing the Moment

Sometimes the door to an opportunity opens through a layoff or unexpected change in circumstances. What was once a pipe dream can suddenly become the most practical thing to do.

ALLISON REILLY AND IAN DOWE

Allison Reilly (45) and Ian Dowe (44) have been married for 20 years and live in Andover, Massachusetts with their children. They have owned their own business, THINKcollaborative, Inc., a marketing communications and advertising agency, for eight years.

Ian: I was working on the marketing side with a budget of $12 million dollars a year, and I was responsible for products totaling $120 million dollars. My job allowed Allison to stop working and focus on our personal and home life.

Allison: This business came about because Ian lost his job. He couldn't find a new one, and I was ready. We thought, "Why don't we do this? Why don't we try? We have nothing to lose." We had talked about having our own business one day, possibly a family business. But we hadn't had a great vision of what it might be, so it wasn't just about having our own advertising agency. We had even talked about buying a bar in Cambridge called The Plough and Stars!

Ian: I lost my job at the worst possible time, at the beginning of the recession. It was a very frustrating year and a half going through that process, not knowing when it was going to end, but knowing that I had to do something. I even contemplated completely shifting careers.

Allison: We were lucky. Right from the beginning we got an account, so we didn't need financing. We were able to get it going, and then we got more and more business. It was a great beginning.

Ian: Over a three-hour breakfast and numerous cups of coffee, Allison and I just started throwing ideas out there — individual ideas and collective ones, discussing what we wanted out of the business, and where we could take it.

Allison: It's evolved from there. Now we identify and sell ourselves under the company name, and we collaborate with other professionals as we need them. We also have a mission statement and a vision of who we are, which we were unaware of when we first started.

If At First You Don't Succeed…
The business idea that reflects a deep and abiding passion may not be practical. Business failures and learning from those mistakes can lead to a perfect combination of practicality and enjoyment in your daily work lives.

JACK AND JOYCE ZIMMERMAN

Jack (67) and Joyce (65) Zimmerman have been married for 43 years. At the time of our interview, they were the co-owners of Home Spirits, a successful full-line liquor store with an emphasis on great local wines from Massachusetts. However, it was not their first business venture; in fact, Jack said that they had been in business together for "a lifetime!"

Jack: We've been in this business for a couple of years. This is actually our second venture where we work together on a daily basis. For many years, while raising a family, I was primarily in business and Joyce was home with our four kids. We had a Jewish book business and it was a disaster.

With some decisions you look back and say, "Well, we took the wrong road, or we made a bad decision." And there are others where you look back and say, "What were we thinking?" The book business was one of those. I was not working at the time and looking for something, and Joyce was a Judaic artist. So our premise seemed to make sense, but it was misguided. We eventually liquidated it after a couple of years.

The Zimmermans have since sold Home Spirits and retired to upstate New York, where their children and grandchildren live. They own and manage 11 units in three apartment buildings and are still in business together!

Joyce: I enjoyed educating our customers about fine wines and making a profit too! Now, after many years, I enjoy spending time in my studio, happily creating art.

Growing a Big Business

How do you build a thriving global business? You have a goal, stay focused and step by step pay attention to opportunities that present themselves to you. And then you make your strategic moves.

MEL AND LINDA SHAPIRO

Mel (82) and Linda (72) Shapiro have been married almost 40 years and live in the suburbs of New York City. Together they have three grown daughters and seven grandchildren. This is a second marriage for both. They began their business 42 years ago and recently sold it. While he was working at a company called Lafayette Radio, Mel started a marine electronics business. During that time Linda was studying with Martha Graham in NYC, and had been a student and teacher of modern dance. After seven or eight years, Mel sold his interest in his marine electronics business to Lafayette Radio and started Terramar Sports Worldwide, Ltd. with Linda.

Mel: I was at a London boat show; I got interested in foul weather gear for sailing and I started by representing a company out of Scotland. I was still selling clothing for sailing when I brought Linda into the company and started full time with Terramar. I always had an interest in clothing and I liked the marine industry. I thought this was something I could bring Linda into since I knew everyone in the marine field and I could introduce a clothing line to them. We had a built-in customer base.

Linda: In the mid-70s we developed a line of rugged sportswear called Grassroots. We kept adding to the line for the outdoor industry.

Mel: At some point we gave up the marine products and focused on the outdoor industry, selling to backpacking, ski and camping stores throughout the country. Eddie Bauer was one of our first customers.

Linda: Mel did not want to work for a corporation. He was entrepreneurial and wanted his own business.

Mel: At the beginning, I just wanted to do something for myself — to start a business and actually grow it into a big business.

Linda: A key turning point was when Nixon opened up trade with China. We got into China early in 1980, and we were able to get silk at very reasonable prices. Before then, people were getting silk from Italy and it was very costly. That moment was a major turning point in our company. It was a four or five year transition.

Mel: We were the first company to import thermal silk underwear from mainland China, which provides virtually 99% of the world's silk. We introduced a line of silk underwear to the outdoor trade.

Linda: Up until that point, we were doing okay; we were managing, but our products were not that much different from others. Silk was a new hot thing for the ski industry and it got us a presence in the marketplace.

Mel: Like any good businessman, you go where the opportunities are. And when China came along as a source for competitively priced and well made items we felt that was where we should focus our attention. At that point we gave up the rugged sportswear — which was becoming fashion driven and required a lot of design work — and we focused the company on the base layer, which is underwear.

Linda: It was good for the business and for the relationship. In every business there is one product that gets it going: for Terramar it was Thermasilk. It was the beginning of our being able to fulfill his vision. It was the success of his vision that allowed us to sell the company.

Motivating Force 2: Tradition

A number of couples grow up in entrepreneurial families or their business interests are encouraged by family traditions. Other couples make choices distinct from their families', thereby creating new customs which honor their parents' unexpressed values and unfulfilled dreams. Family tradition is carried out in many ways beyond taking over a family business, including being business and entrepreneurial minded.

Like My Father Before Me

There are times when opportunity, interest and ability coincide, and you are called upon to follow in a parent's footsteps. The challenge is to bring your own strengths, ingenuity and creativity to the task. This next couple is one example of the powerful effect of family tradition.

SANDY AND JEFFREY DAVIS

Co-executives Jeffrey (55) and Sandy (52) Davis were inspired by their entrepreneurial father and stepfather. Jeffrey is founder and CEO of Mage, LLC, a business consulting firm that provides strategic advice to entrepreneurs and family businesses. As co-founder of the Family Business Association, he currently teaches entrepreneurship at Babson College Graduate School, and co-hosts the syndicated daily radio show "*Mind Your Own Business*" (MYOB).

As President of both HRG Development, Inc., and Boston Catering Connection, Inc., Sandy manages both the real estate portfolio and financial investments for her family's trust. They have been together for fourteen years and married for eight. Separately and collectively they have owned or been involved with ten or more businesses. Here is their complex business story.

Sandy: My father, Harvey R. Goldstein, was an incredibly successful entrepreneur who died seventeen years ago. He was involved with many different businesses and was quite successful in land development and the family's manufacturing business.

Jeffrey: Sandy had owned three restaurants when I met her and had degrees in culinary arts and hotel management. She ran the original training store for Boston Chicken. I was impressed with her varied experiences when I first met her. She also owned an event planning and off-premise catering business that represented twelve different restaurants around town.

With this business model, she didn't have overhead; the restaurants didn't have to hire management or staff, and a customer could have a party with tastings from each of the restaurants. It wasn't until nine years ago that Sandy went into her father's business, after we had some discussions about her reasserting herself in her family's estate.

Sandy: Among those family members who held board positions in the family business, which was called Pioneer Cover-All, I was the only one with business experience. However, the manufacturing business was completely foreign to me, and the construction and refuse end of the business did not have many women involved.

Back in 1963, my father had the brainstorm idea when he was driving and saw debris falling from the back of trucks, and he said, "Someday there are going to be laws against this." Later, he found an engineer to develop the first automated truck cover system patent to solve this environmental issue. The most popular patent, the rack and pinion cover, led to sole supplier contracts with BFI and Allied Waste Management.

Jeffrey: There isn't a day in Massachusetts that you don't see a refuse truck going down the street with a Pioneer Cover-All rack and pinion cover on it — it's the one with hydraulic arms that takes a tarpaulin on and off the truck. It's important to give your father credit. He is a legend to this day, the type of man you could write a whole book about.

Sandy was so close with her father that her mother says she *is* her father. When he passed away, the smallest part of his portfolio was this business. Sandy always believed that it had immense potential and put pressure on the board to release that potential. At one point there was a political struggle and they voted her off the board. She worked to get back on the board; years later she became the president of the company and it skyrocketed under her leadership.

Sandy: I have to acknowledge the support from my husband and my mother, as well as the dedication of the trustees and loyal company employees during the tough times. The company's sales doubled, and when the market timing was right, the business was sold at a premium. It was a great accomplishment.

Simultaneously, I inherited the management of all of my father's real estate and business holdings. The parent business was named HRG, after my father's initials. It took a lot of time to learn the manufacturing business because it involved an ongoing factory that needed day-to-day attention. At the same time, I was trying to get a handle on the real estate portfolio and not let that go unattended. I've found a way to get support to strike a good balance between my role as president of two corporations and managing multiple partnerships, including the family trust.

Focus on Money

Profitability is at the heart of a successful business. Learning to appreciate having money is one thing we can learn from our families, but learning to enjoy using money is another. How couples use the money they have is an ongoing negotiation.

WENDY CAPLAND AND CHRIS MICHAUD

Wendy Capland (55) and Chris Michaud (59) have been married for fifteen years. They are parents of grown children from their first marriages. Wendy, a certified master coach, holds a dual Master's degree in counseling and business management. She has been self-employed since 1987. Founder and CEO of VisionQuest Consulting, she is a highly successful leadership development expert. Chris, a licensed real estate broker, was in business for himself for 22 years before he took a break to spend four years learning about the world of technology. He worked with Wendy for several of those years, and has now re-entered the market with his own real estate company.

Wendy: I grew up in a family of entrepreneurs. My dad's family owned a leather tannery company, and over the years he became successful, sold businesses and made money. Even though I didn't feel like we had a lot of money in those days, as a young adult that started to change. I think that experience definitely had an impact on me.

Chris: When I worked with Wendy, I contributed to her business by influencing things at the board of directors' level to help make and keep her profitable. I believe you should plan for profitability like anything else. Most small entrepreneurs don't calculate that. They hope for a profit, but they don't plan for it. When I ran a real estate office, I was known for my frugality and my profitability in an area of the state of Maine where small entrepreneurs have been known to struggle. Wendy is the detail-oriented person and I'm the visionary with regard to profitability, in that I consistently remind her of what she needs to look at to maintain her profitability.

Wendy: We come from very different backgrounds. Chris's family lives simply; mine, a little more extravagantly. It doesn't seem to bother us either way. He keeps me real regarding money. And I help him spend it!

Chris: That's true, and it's actually quite a skill to balance the two. Wendy has taught me that it's okay to spend money.

A Gift from the Past Becomes the Present
Parents give us the gift of life and the gift of deeply held values. It is up to us to choose the way we want to express our inherited values.

JOHN WITTY AND ELLYN SPRAGINS

John Witty (58) and Ellyn Spragins (57) are a creative couple exploring new paths in their professions as journalists and writers. They have chosen very different work lives from those of their families, with a new vision for moving into the future. Ellyn is a keynote speaker, author and owner of What I Know Now™ Enterprises and a former contributing editor at *Fortune Small Business*. Her book, *What I Know Now—Letters to My Younger Self*, is a collection of insights and sage advice from famous women to their younger selves. John is a financial writer.

Ellyn: There was no obvious role model in my family so John and I progressed in our careers, navigating as independents. My dad was a Major General in the Army, and even though he was in this highly structured traditional organization, he was a very creative thinker and experimenter. He is a perennial optimist and enthusiastic about new ideas. Also, I remember my mom telling me at a young age that I could do anything I wanted. She had a career as a housewife, and she had never completed college. Although neither modeled the creative, independent, entrepreneurial, freelance kind of life we have taken up, they each had deeply held values that my choices reflect.

My connection with my mom is very direct. When she died, I started to think about what I wished I had known or wished she would have told me if she had looked back at her own life. I was a little slow to waking up to this idea, but then I realized it was a great idea for a book and it was meant for me to do, not just think about. That was a profound turning point for me. Not just because it was connected to my mother, but because for the first time a project was so personally adapted to me — because of how I conceived of it, and also because I am very empathetic. I can understand the emotional typography when someone is talking to me — I enter into their world. The whole book and everything that ensued has been more satisfying than anything that came before.

John: This was true in my circumstances as well. I grew up in one of those small New England mill towns. Orange, Massachusetts was a fabulous place to grow up in the 50s and 60s and still is a wonderful little place. Now families with a lot of money or sophistication live there.

But when I grew up I didn't have a sophisticated upbringing. My parents were wonderful people with a small-town world vision. My father was the lawyer in town and had a monopoly on the legal business, so I had some status in a small town, which was enjoyable and has affected the way I've lived my life. But the way in which my parents lived and their relationship are not the way Ellyn and I relate to each other or how we live our lives. We continue to create our relationship and our lives, with an awareness of the influence of the larger world.

Motivating Force 3: Vision

A vision can keep you up at night, can wake you up in the morning energized for the entire day and, in some cases, can inspire you for a lifetime. It is a driving force and if you're lucky, the vision won't leave you alone until it gets your attention and active response.

As couples get to know each other, they discover that they share visions for themselves, their relationship and the world. They can derive great pleasure from sharing, discussing, planning and implementing their visions. Vision can provide the motivation to honor their entrepreneurial spirits, and, with or without a full-blown plan, can allow them to follow their desires and take those critical first steps to act on a business idea.

Family Relationships and "Millions of Leaders"

Being driven by strong values that are embedded in both the business and the marriage empowers a couple's partnership and can make a powerful difference in their business, family and community.

ALAN PRICE AND GINA LAROCHE

Values about family relationships and the vision of "millions of leaders" infuse the success of this leadership consulting team. Gina LaRoche (45) and Alan Price (48) are a business couple residing in New Haven, Connecticut. Married for eighteen years, they are the parents of two sons, Jackson (15) and Griffin (13). Graduates of Harvard Business School and Harvard Law School respectively, they have led varied work lives in corporate America and in academia. Gina had her own business first. At the time of our interview they had founded their own leadership consulting firm, Inspiritas, Inc. Gina has gone on to be a co-founder of Seven Stones Leadership, Inc., and Alan, the author of *Are You Ready to Lead? A Story for Leaders and Their Mentors*, is currently Manager of Organizational Effectiveness at Northeast Utilities.

Gina: Alan pushed me to leave corporate America and start my own business. Once I did that, I had the confidence to start another. I just had a sense that we could go into business together and be good at it.

Alan: We had a vision and mission right out of the block, and we've continued to adjust it. More than being an entrepreneur, the vision of "millions of leaders" spoke to me. I wrote my book as a contribution to them.

Gina: The vision of "millions of leaders over the next century" has always been our guiding principle.

Alan: Marriage comes first. Even though we talk about business all the time — 80/20 talking about business vs. talking about marriage — I'd walk away from the business in a heartbeat if I felt it was incompatible with my marriage. I am devoted to my family. My vision of life is to stay married to Gina and spend time together happily, enjoying the world of ideas, traveling and raising a wonderful family, exposing them to the physical world and the world of ideas. We have talents that we are bringing to bear in Inspiritas, Inc. — talents for training and developing millions of leaders. I love that vision and I walk a path where I am able to contribute to leaders every day. I want my life to have meaning, to make a difference.

Gina: I'm similar. I am inspired when I know that I made a difference in someone's life. Our vision for the company is showing people that they have leadership capacity within them. We will help them get to a new level, both individually and as part of an organization. We will do all that in the environment of our own company, which values our family and our freedom. We would like to see more of that type of lifestyle through-out corporate America.

I don't think either of us really believes we are going to be doing what we are doing ten years from now. Not that we necessarily won't be doing it, but we're not sitting here thinking about ten years from now, or twenty years from now. I think if anything we have a five year horizon.

I never really thought about a vision for our marriage. I think, ulti-mately, I see us as 60 years old and living in some town somewhere off the grid, writing and teaching at the local college. I do see us still working together: either we're both writers and authors, or we both teach — even if Alan runs for public office — we are working together and happily married.

Consciously Responsible for the Next Seven Generations

Some couples develop a vision for their business based on the purpose of their couple partnership. They create a business that thoroughly captures their vision and leadership legacy.

SUZANNE AND DWIGHT FRINDT

Suzanne (54) and Dwight (67) Frindt, business leaders and global citizens, are co-founders and principals of 2130 Partners, an organiza-tion founded in 1990 to develop "leadership for generations." They have been married for over 20 years in a second marriage for both, and they are the parents of four children and the grandparents of two children.

Suzanne: Before we married, before we had our business together, we started with thirty conversations we would have during our evening walk, asking questions such as, "What is the purpose of being married?" or "What is the synergistic opportunity of us as a couple, versus two highly accomplished individuals connecting in a personal relationship?" Through those thirty conversations we generated a vision statement for our couple partnership that looked at how the synergy of our couple partnership would manifest in 2130, 140 years from now. We called it S&D Partners 2130. We were asking ourselves how our being a couple would positively impact the world for many generations beyond our time, when people no longer remembered our names, and there were no statues and no plaques to our memory.

Dwight: We tried to imagine what people in 2130 would want us to devote our lives to if they could tell us, even though they wouldn't even know we existed, or that our kids existed.

Dwight: We are both MBAs, so naturally we thought we needed a business plan for our relationship. We borrowed from the Native American view of accountability, where the leaders are consciously responsible for their impact on each of the next seven generations.

Suzanne: This viewpoint was pivotal for us and the foundation for everything we did in our business. We came up with our own personal vision/mission statement for influencing resources and resourcefulness in such a way that each and every person on the planet would have the opportunity for a healthy and productive life. We thought that idea was worth focusing our couple partnership on, personally and professionally. We knew from previous marriages that when the going gets tough, it takes more than a piece of paper or a judge, priest or minister to tell us you're married and this is the way it has to be. Our commitment and practices have kept us fulfilling on this vision.

Dreams, Values and Making a Difference
We all have the possibility of boldly and courageously living out our highest purposes or destiny. When we exercise that option over time, miraculous things often occur that shift our personal and societal reality.

ANNE AND CHRISTOPHER ELLINGER
Anne (55) and Christopher (54) Ellinger are strongly led by their dreams and values. They originally connected with the transformative power of the arts through their work with Playback Theatre, and also founded their

own troupe called True Story Theater. Since then they have promoted the field of Social Healing Arts through their Arts Rising project and by initiating the Playback North America network. They also share a background in philanthropy and wealth counseling as the founders of More Than Money, and, more recently, Bolder Giving, whose philanthropic mission, by providing remarkable role models and practical support, is to inspire people at every economic level to give at their full potential.

Anne and Christopher met in an idealistic project that articulated values of simple living and social activism. As the years went by, they developed ways to act on these values in partnership. Their vision reflects their shared values, the driving force for their many business ventures. These values are integrated into all aspects of their life together.

Christopher: A big factor was meeting each other at a leadership training center in Philadelphia, where we also met people decades older than we were who claimed "working for social change" as their profession. Their stories gave us faith that even a very small project could make a huge difference, that we didn't have to go join a big company or corporation to be effective.

Anne: Being there when we were both in our early twenties was a life-changing experience — formative to our values, our partnership and our work.

In July of 2010, the Ellingers' "Bolder Giving" project was awarded a three-year $675,000 challenge grant by the Bill & Melinda Gates Foundation. With this support, Bolder Giving will expand its efforts to collect and share inspiring stories of courageous donors. Bolder Giving's tagline is "Give more. Risk more. Inspire more." The project encourages people not only to give more money, as a percentage of income or assets, but also to risk more in where and how they give, and to inspire more by being public about their giving. The stories on Bolder Giving's website helped inspire the Billionaire's Giving Pledge, whose 57 signers to date have committed $220 billion to charitable causes.

Anne: At a time when mounting challenges are facing our families, communities, country and world, the need is critical for people to give boldly to help meet these challenges. Not only is courageous and engaged giving essential for the world, it also brings tremendous personal fulfillment to those who give.

Vision Defined, Vision in Process

Many couples finance their business out of savings, loans and their own ongoing work. **John Witty and Ellyn Spragins** [p. 15] describe how this can work well when one partner is enrolled in the other's vision and lends support as they bring their business to life.

Ellyn: My vision has really grown and changed over time. My vision is to put ten years into making What I Now Know Enterprises into a highly profitable business that offers products and services to support women and their life wisdom. During those ten years I will be introducing some key elements into my life — like learning about and engaging in art and becoming an artist — that will then play out more fully by the end of that time, when I can continue to own my business, but work as little or as much as I would like. John is really crucial to this vision of our lives and our relationship — he's been a key element in everything I've done. I envision him as a big part of this growing company that will be individually beneficial for both of us, and a shared experience that will stretch the boundaries of what we know how to do.

John: My orientation is to develop a company called "What I've Never Known" (Laughter) And Will Never Know Again!" My vision of where my writing and journalism career is taking me is less defined than Ellyn's. Two things: Ellyn is a seasoned professional journalist and has been at it a lot longer than I have. I don't have her passion or vision for that stuff. I love working for Merrill Lynch. I think it's a great gig because it's just three miles from my house. However, I am way down at the bottom of the ladder looking up so many pant legs and dresses — metaphorically speaking! But that doesn't bother me because we both make a comfortable living doing what we do. I'm all for Ellyn's expansion of her great ideas and efforts with books and authorship. I am eager to see where she takes it, and also where I can get involved in expanding the brand and the public's knowledge of her as an author.

A well articulated vision calls to others who share the same values and commitments. People are drawn to support and participate in a vision that resonates with and expands their own vision. Also, people who are driven by vision are inspired by and attracted to like-minded people, so you may find others in your community and networks joining you as you begin bringing your vision to life.

Motivating Force 4: Mission

Mission is the compelling desire and the driving force in creating the future. Mission is often expressed as a powerful and focused statement of purpose and beliefs. Who are we going to serve? What does our organization stand for? A strong mission shines through the stories of these next couples.

From Life-Threatening to Life-Giving

Some entrepreneurs are motivated by a crisis that becomes a driving mission to help others in similar circumstances.

MARGUERITE PIRET AND RICHARD ROSEN

Married over 40 years, Marguerite Piret (61) and Richard Rosen (71) have extensive experience as executives in their own companies. Marguerite is CEO of Newbury Piret, an investment banking business. Richard is a true entrepreneur who has been the leader of several companies. He thrives on the many challenges he has taken on during his 42 years of executive experience. He described a life-threatening experience in 1999 that got him into action in developing Diagnostic, Inc., a new company in the field of medical technology.

Richard: I have low vision as a result of a serious infection. This particular experience put me in contact with the medical profession, and I was horrified by what I saw. I decided I would do something that I had worried about a long time ago when I used to teach a course in medical decision-making at Harvard Medical School. Together with a good friend of mine who's a professor at MIT, I conceived of a company to transform the care of chronic disease from episodic care to continuous care, and to do something rather far-reaching in medical terms: to rely not on typical aggregated data, which is the convention of medicine, but to rely on individualized care that uses only "Mrs. Jones's" data to do her treatment. This is a big deal.

We are implementing that now, and we have a very large backlog. I think this company is going to become a pretty big company. Now what happens to the company, I can't say. It's a function of the cards that get dealt to you. A month ago, I never thought of doing business in Malaysia. Then the Malaysian government came to us and said they were interested in what we were doing, and asked us to take care of their one million diabetics, to tailor and design a system. That's a billion dollar opportunity.

Marguerite: This is an important commentary, because in the United States we have so many insurance companies and so many payers that it's very difficult to innovate. It's much easier to deal with a nationalized medical care system.

Commitment to Environmental Sustainability, Spiritual Fulfillment and Social Justice

Some couples work side by side in their individual businesses as they support one another to live out their dreams. Then a series of unexpected events can bring them together in a joint venture that expresses both of their missions. This next couple went through a startling and empowering transformation in their working relationship. He was the successful businessman and she was the designated global activist until he took on the mantle of primary driver for their global activism. Their story is one of a mission realized.

LYNNE AND BILL TWIST

Lynne (65) and Bill (67) Twist are long-time San Franciscans. Married for over forty years, they have three grown children and four grandchildren. Lynne is the author of the highly acclaimed book, *The Soul of Money: Transforming Your Relationship with Money and Life.* While they have brought their talents and skills together in everything they do, it wasn't until 12 years ago that the Twists launched their current business venture. The story of how they came to create what they called "The Pachamama Alliance" is a fascinating one.

Lynne: We've been in service or working together in some way or another for a long time. We started Pacific Primary, a nursery school, in 1974, when our children were two, four and six. I was really the founder of the school, but I roped Bill into doing all the financial stuff because he's a financial genius. He became the president, and we called him "The Chancellor." If Bill is involved in something, it will be stable, sound and financially secure. I can inspire and enroll everybody, and I can raise the money, but he manages the operation.

I started working for The Hunger Project in 1977. Bill was a very successful businessman at the time, making lots of money and traveling a lot.

Bill: I was specifically in equipment leasing for the transportation industry — airplanes, railroads, ships, big capital equipment items.

Lynne: As The Hunger Project got bigger and more complicated, it became obvious that it would be really good to get Bill involved in the whole financial thing. So he became president of the U.S. board, the chief financial officer for our global operations as a volunteer, and we were big contributors. Yet it was really Bill's productivity in his business that made it all possible. He ended up being a partner to me in The Hunger Project for the twenty years I was on staff.

When we were first invited to go to Ecuador with the Achuar tribe, I had to talk him into going — it was an adventure but we really didn't know what we were getting into.

Bill: We started working together in earnest when Pachamama was created. We actually ended up being involved in something together where we had to make decisions together and work out issues so that we were aligned on how things were going to go.

Lynne: In fact, we had a bit of a hard time working together.

Interviewer: It was the first time you began to test certain ways of being together outside the domain of being together as husband and wife or as parents, and the other ways you'd already been together up to that point.

Lynne: Exactly. And I admit we had some rough patches with that. I would not want to tell him things because he was the financial guy. He sometimes seemed like a constraining force to me. We almost went our separate ways inside The Hunger Project. Our work inside The Pachamama Alliance is completely different.

Bill: Calling it a business is a little funny, but it works. The Pachamama Alliance is a business whose purpose is organic and evolving. It started out pretty clearly as an environmentally-oriented enterprise, working on environmental issues in Latin America. As it began growing, it became clear that it's not just environmental: it's human rights oriented. It's also obvious now that it's not just for Latin America.

For me, the business is now something that aligns with my vision. We stand for a conscious and intentional human presence on the planet that is oriented toward people's relationship with life. That vision is very much tied in with my personal vision.

Lynne: Even though I instigated our contact with the Achuar and organized the first trip, when we were in the rainforest and had our first profound encounter with the Achuar people, the idea of The Pachama-ma Alliance really got into Bill's soul in a way that I didn't at all expect. While it also got into mine, Bill emerged from that experience as the leader of the initiative. I then stood behind him. I would say that The Hunger Project was mine and he stood behind me with money, time, energy, love, advice, wisdom and with participation. The Pachamama Alliance really ended up being his calling; then I got totally into part-nership with him, stood behind him and with him. But I feel like it's his turn for deciding what our lives are about.

A Promise Kept

Sustained by a transformative vision, a specific business goal and a com-mitment to an influential mentor, a couple can make and keep a big promise to themselves and to the world. While you can have a nascent vision, a mentor can ignite a fire that keeps burning brightly long after you're both gone.

NICK AND MITRA LORE

Nick (66) and Mitra Mortazavi (57) Lore live near Washington, DC. This is a second marriage for each of them. Nick began his business thirty years ago with a big vision: to transform the business of career counseling and be the best in the world. His wife Mitra, who had varied business experience in ladies accessories and real estate, joined the busi-ness after their marriage twenty years ago. Rockport Institute is now well-known for successfully coaching mid-career professionals through the process of career change, and for guiding young people to make the best choices for their education and career path.

Nick: Our commitment from the very beginning was to be the best in the world. I don't think there's anything extraordinary about us. Ca-reer counseling was so primitive and so basic that it wasn't difficult. Rockport has created many of the methods used today by leading-edge career counseling professionals, and has brought the art of choosing a fulfilling career into the 21st century. We offer programs and services to people of all ages and situations. Clients have one thing in common: a desire to make a career choice that will be highly satisfying and lead to maximum success.

I was twenty-seven years old and searching for an adult career. I managed a factory. That went well, and I ended up running other businesses. I wound up living on the coast of Maine, and was fortunate enough to make friends with Buckminster Fuller. We belonged to the same little Maine yacht club and he became my coach, helping me look at what I was going to do. I wanted to do a lifelong project that made a difference in people's lives, where I could make a big contribution, but I questioned whether I was smart enough. I looked for career counselors to get some more specific help in some of the areas that Bucky really didn't know anything about.

In talking to these counselors all around New England, I realized that they didn't seem to know what they were talking about. Their whole model of who people are and what it is to have a life that you love was so constricted. It all came together then, as I realized that nobody had taken on career as a form of self-expression. People in the 60s talked about self-expression, but they would say, "Well, just do what Joseph Campbell suggests and 'follow your bliss'." What exactly does bliss mean? It was all sort of amorphous. I decided that I would delve into it and completely reinvent career coaching from the ground up, and that's what Rockport did.

I made promises to Bucky. They included developing a methodology that worked, that people could, by using it, choose careers that were a great fit. I also promised to alter society's conversation so that people actually knew that they could do something they loved, and that the tools they needed were part of the culture and accessible to them. Rockport grew out of those promises. A few years ago, I completed the last promise to Bucky. In 1998 I wrote a book called *The Pathfinder: How to Choose or Change Your Career for a Lifetime of Satisfaction and Success.* Then, in 2008, I wrote a similar book for young people, *Now What?: The Young Person's Guide to Choosing the Perfect Career,* in response to our feeling called to work with them.

Intersecting Motivations
Some couples consciously connect two or more motivations for going into business together right from the start. The layering of practicality and family history with being passionate about a vision or a mission makes for a rich and complex work life.

Bridging the Vision and the Plan
This couple's parents were friends, but they didn't meet each other until they were adults. Lifelong business owners with a commitment to Africa,

they envisioned a practical and profitable way to partner with women in Kenya to develop sustainable enterprises and create thriving businesses. Their creative talents, combined with a love of the natural world and their mutual commitment to service, gave rise to a business that stirs the human heart with compassion and wonder.

PHILIP AND KATY LEAKEY

Philip (62) and Katy (57) Leakey's story is an unusual one. Katy's parents, Mr. and Mrs. Robert Moody, were cofounders of the Leakey Foundation, which recognized and supported the work of his parents, the archaeologists Louis and Mary Leakey. As a child, Katy met Philip's parents in the 60s, but didn't meet Philip for the first time until the 1980s when they were both in their early thirties. They married in 2001 and started in business together in 2002. In their current business, The Leakey Collection, which is based in central Kenya, Philip and Katy combine their talents in interior design and the arts with their love of nature to develop stunning handcrafted products for an international market. Using natural elements such as fallen wood, grass and ceramic, these renowned designers create unique products while protecting the environment and providing economic opportunity for the local communities.

Philip: Immediately before we got together, I was involved in raising the understanding about Kenya in the halls of American academia.

Katy: For twenty years, I had a mural business in Colorado and California, specializing in commercial real estate and working with architects from the ground up. My fine arts career was influenced by Philip's family connection with The Leakey Foundation. When I became interested in cultural anthropology and what connects us as species, I studied in South America. I was also lecturing at various universities with a mission very similar to Philip's: to make America more open to other cultures.

Philip: Our business came about as a consequence of our need and desire to help our neighbors. We live in the bush in Kenya amidst the Maasai people, and most of the people, especially the women, have never had a cash economy. During 2000, Kenya experienced a severe drought that lasted for two years, and things got pretty desperate for the women. The men had gone off looking for grazing and left the women and children behind with few goods and no means of support. Some became destitute and started coming to our home to look for help. We gave them money and food. When it came to about a hundred families, we asked ourselves how we could create some work for them so that they could have dignity and avert disaster in the future. Beading is their main skill. They have a lot of experience in it — you've seen the fantastic jewelry they wear. We thought about how we could convert that skill into a contemporary product that could find a market in the U.S., Europe and the rest of the Western world. Beads are expensive, and that led us to wonder how we could create a bead that isn't.

I have been very involved in using plants in my business for a variety of purposes, so I was familiar with a grass that I had previously used in the furniture business. We turned that grass into beads. When we tested it on the market, people were interested and it took off from there. In a short time we had enough women working so that when the next drought came, four years later, no one was suffering. We fulfilled our desire to help people live with dignity, and fulfilled their need to have a sustainable income for the first time in their lives.

Here was our biggest challenge. We never wanted to disturb their culture, their way of life. We didn't want to set up any factories. We wanted to keep it a simple process that they could participate in. We developed a system where they could come anytime they liked. Whether they came one day a year or six days a week or two hours a day, they would still be put to work. In their lifestyle, they have a lot of demands — ceremonies and the like. They could disappear for a ceremony for two months at a time, which makes for an interesting challenge in having reliable production.

So the challenge was to connect an unreliable production chain to this side of the world where there is a highly demanding consumer base — retailers are exacting and they want things on time. But we've managed to develop a system that has been very successful. We now have 1,400 women in the rural areas in Kenya making this jewelry, and we have about 2,000 stores in the U.S. We only sell wholesale so we are the bridge between them. We see it as a model, and the possibility for expanding it is phenomenal.

Joining two dramatically different cultures in this way creates a profound shift, which is not only about a business created by an extraordinarily creative entrepreneurial couple, but also about creating a prototype for conducting business in the developing world that is flexible, workable and profitable.

Mission and Practicality: Discovering Resources within the Relationship

There are often untapped resources within a relationship that surface only when necessity calls the couple to bring them forward. When the wife in this relationship needed her husband's practical skills, he joined her in the business. Practical need and mission-driven motivations came together to benefit both their relationship and their business.

SHERRI AND TERRY MCARDLE

Sherri (52) and Terry (59) McArdle have been a couple for 34 years and married for 30. They met at work in downtown Manhattan at the US Life Insurance Company, where he was a supervisor and she a work co-op student. Years later, when Terry joined McArdle Ramerman, Inc., the business Sherri had started with her business partner, Jim, the tables were turned. They spoke about their mission.

Sherri: Our mission? To enhance organizational vitality by engaging leaders at all levels in engaging their people. Together with our clients we discover, create and achieve breakthrough results as we advance the practice of strategic leadership and organizational transformation. That is why we are here: to fulfill this passionate cause. It's the excitement we wake up to every morning.

I worked for a small consulting firm for the first few years to get my feet wet. That's where I met my business partner, Jim Ramerman, who enjoyed the team aspect of business as much as I did.

Starting a business is daunting for most people, but it was second nature for me. There was no beginning hurdle of "Can I do this?" — it was a natural extension of who I am. Others asked, "Didn't that take a lot of courage?" I would say sure but for me, not really. I know this is what I was born to do — to be on my own and independent. Jim and I had some good jobs when we started, and we developed a good practice. Now we are developing a great business and bringing in additional people.

Terry: I am a lot happier working for Sherri and Jim than I have ever been before and I've worked for my own mother. My mom ran a weekly

newspaper in Queens and I was in a role very similar to the one I'm fulfilling here: elevating the business practices of the business by setting up
the human, technology and process systems so they work as efficiently
as possible. My aim is to have the functionality of each person in the
firm improve with training. This is a natural calling for me, so I get to do
what I really love to do.

Sherri: The mission of the business is an extension of my own personal
mission. I literally feel privileged to get up and do this work every day.
Terry's joining the business has added immensely to our relationship.
We now share this phenomenal vision together, each of us contributing
in our own way. It's given us more in common. We brought diversity
into our workplaces before we worked together. But now Terry is part of
building this great organization and we can it do together. That gives us
something to talk about, which is another really good thing 30 years into
a marriage!

Vision and Partnership: Whatever We Do, We Do Together

SCOTT AND SUE RICHARDSON

Scott (50) and Sue (47) Richardson have been married for twenty
years and in business together for more than ten years. They have a
daughter, Sophie (6) and live in the suburbs of Boston, Massachusetts.
Longwood Software, Inc. is their own service provider company, which
caters to marketing departments in corporations with revenues of $50
million or more.

Scott: Right from the beginning, I wanted to be a business guy. That's
what I was all about. My dad worked for CBS News as a journalist
and later as an upper level manager of the news division, so we were
wired into the world of government and politics. For me, though, the
choice was always business. It offered me the opportunity to work with
both technology and people. I have an MBA, but rather than go to Wall
Street, I wanted to keep things simple and straightforward by creating a
company that made a product.

Sue: As the wife of an entrepreneurial spouse, I was by definition involved from the beginning. More than that, though, I chose to support
Scott in the business by being on the board.

Scott: We were very close, and she was always a tremendous resource and support for me. She came onto the board because we wanted to be involved as a family.

Our vision for the business is to offer a fundamental set of tools that our customers can use every day to be more productive. Along the way we want to build an asset that can be sold to another company, and that will source our next adventure, which includes spending time with our child. Our vision for our life is that whatever we're going to do, we're going to do together. The business is both a means to an end and an end in and of itself, because it's a platform for us to be and work together.

Sue: Scott has talked about the possibility of being a teacher at some point beyond this business. Eventually, we would like to combine our efforts into community business consulting.

Practical Visionaries: Sharing Power

It can be lonely at the top when you bear the full weight of responsibility. One practical benefit of sharing responsibility with someone you trust implicitly is the balance of power in the relationship. If you share a vision, you will find in each other a powerful ally.

CLAUDETTE AND ADE FAISON

Claudette (56) and Ade (66) Faison are the creator and co-owner, respectively, of New York Youth at Risk, an organization whose mission is to transform the lives of at-risk youth and families in New York City.

Claudette: Money was part of it, but not all of it. The vision was strong and bigger than me, and I couldn't get it done alone. There was a sense of being defeated or up against something and always being vulnerable "out there." Having Ade join me provided the security of having someone who understood and was committed to the vision, which eliminated some of that discomfort.

We're dedicated to expanding our capacity to reach young people and high-risk families in New York City and the surrounding area, as well as consulting to other Youth At Risk organizations in this country and in other countries. The latest effort is to launch an Internet-based knowledge asset that captures all of what we do in video and audio form. It documents the knowledge we have so that people can access this work and learn from it in order to perform it in their host city.

As managers of the program, it allows us to virtually stand in front of young people without actually having to go there.

Working in law firms taught me that whoever brings in the most money has the power. Being the female, and the founder, and the person that generated the income that paid both our salaries didn't work for the relationship. I was in the typical "man" position, and I didn't really want to be the provider.

I don't think that position works for me in the business arena either. In the last two-and-a-half years, as Ade has been generating income in the business, I have noticed that I listen differently to him now because there's a real partnership.

Our Perspective on Answering the Call

Our objective in this chapter has been to introduce the key motivators for couples who choose to go into business together. In telling our own story, we were surprised to realize that the four key motivations we discovered were actually all there, interwoven in an organic way and revealed to us over time. The other couples' stories we shared with you illuminated each motivation, one by one — practical partnership, tradition, vision and mission — and further explored how the motivations can be expressed in combination.

We hope this gives you a chance to reflect on and consider the motivations that will lead or have led to the creation of your own business. In listening to many stories, we realized the importance of honoring the beginning of our journeys and expanding our awareness of the forces at work that drive our creative choices and propel us forward.

We trust that you will see yourself in some of these stories and either honor your desire to get started or feel proud of the fact that you have already begun the wild and wonderful journey of being a couple in business together.

What are *your* motivators?

Chapter Takeaways

1. Name the driving forces that have motivated or are motivating you to start a business.

2. Have a dialogue with your partner about a motivation that you now want to develop or incorporate more fully.

3. Clearly identify your values, vision and mission and discuss what you discover with another entrepreneurial couple.

*"For it is mutual trust, even more than mutual interest,
that holds human associations together."*

—H.L. MENCKEN (1880–1956)
AMERICAN JOURNALIST

CHAPTER TWO

WHAT EACH PARTNER CONTRIBUTES: A LOOK AT ROLES AND BOUNDARIES

T
O BEGIN ANYTHING — A relationship, a business or both — we need a strong desire driven by an idea, a vision or a mission. That strong desire fuels our commitment to get into action and gather the resources we need. As we ready ourselves, we consider the resources of time, money, people and their availability to support us. We analyze what we are willing to risk to begin the business. Then we take a first step forward.

Lon and Sandy Golnick, leaders of family and relationship workshops from whom we'll hear more in our chapter on family, have a useful definition of commitment: "Action in favor of your values." Until you are in action to fulfill your mission or vision, commitment is only an idea. Pema Chödrön, an esteemed American Buddhist teacher, describes the powerful effect of being committed:

> *"You are uncommitted until you encounter a particular way that rings true in your heart and you decide to follow it. In order to go deeper, there has to be a wholehearted commitment… you choose one path and stick to it. Then you let it put you through your changes. Without a commitment, the minute you really begin to hurt, you'll just leave or you'll look for something else."* [1]

All the couples we interviewed made a commitment and took a leap of faith. This chapter looks at the resources of strengths and skills that the

---

[1] Pema Chödrön, *Comfortable with Uncertainty: 108 Teachings on Cultivating Fearlessness and Compassion.* Boston: Shambhala Publications. 2003.

couples have used and developed together. Once your desire is clear, and you identify your own strengths, differences, and roles that support your commitment, consider your networks of family, friends, colleagues and communities that have skills and resources you can call upon. Also consider the boundaries you will set so that your efforts will be sustainable.

Strengths and Differences

Our strengths enable us to be in business together. Some of our most notable strengths are carved out of working with the personal differences and varied skill sets that each partner brings to the relationship and the business.

It is essential that you identify your strengths and acknowledge your partner's strengths. If you don't have all the necessary strengths to be in business, you need to either develop them or find others to complement your own capabilities, talents and skills. What strengths and challenges do each of you bring to the table? How can you best work with your differences and employ them as assets?

Committed Business Partners
This couple is very clear about each other's business strengths, and that recognition has contributed to a highly successful business.

MARK ANDRUS AND STACY MADISON

Mark Andrus and Stacy Madison (both 46), founders of one of Massachusetts' fastest growing businesses, Stacy's Pita Chip Company, were in business for ten out of the fifteen years they had known each other. A couple of years into the business, they were married, but chose to divorce after several years. Although they both moved on to other healthy and happy relationships, they continued to be successful business partners until they sold the business to PepsiCo in 2006.

Mark: It's funny, because I think in the beginning we may have known what our individual strengths were, but we sort of struggled with them. We tried to do everything ourselves. There was a lot of overlap — we weren't really sure about boundaries — and that made it difficult at the start. But I think I realized Stacy's strengths. She's more organized than I am with schedules and meetings, marketing and design, while my strengths are more in the creative ideas behind the food and the flavors. I think we play to each other's strengths now; we're able to separate the aspects of the business so she deals with one and I deal with the other, and it works out really well.

Stacy: Mark deals with everything inside the bag: the product, the quality. I deal with the outside: the packaging, the marketing. Personality-wise he's a very lighthearted person and I enjoy his sense of humor. That also makes it a pleasant work atmosphere. Everybody eats lunch together and it's just funny — the conversations that come up are entertaining. I think that adds a lot to the company. Also, in addition to the existing great products, he keeps making delicious new products.

Mark: With a Master's Degree in social work and a Ph.D. in psychology, we entered the snack food industry. Most people who start a business have business degrees. For Stacy and me, it was a love of entrepreneurship, having similar goals and wanting to be in the food business. I believe that not having a business background has allowed us the freedom to step outside the bounds of popular beliefs about "the right way" to do business. The result is that we have created an entirely different culture and one that's much less corporate.

Stacy: Since we were never part of it, we were never tainted by the rigidity of corporate America. From its inception, it has just been the two of us leading the company. We were living on the West Coast, enjoying a healthy lifestyle and making healthy food that tasted really good. We were both always foodies. Mark is a great cook; he would prepare a dish with fresh herbs and fresh fish that was unlike anything I ever ate. We kept talking about how to turn our passion into a business that would be a part of us, reflect who we are and what we love.

Mark: I had always wanted to be a chef. Everyone's a doctor in my family, so they encouraged me to take that route. Once I got my doctorate I said, "Now I can do something that I want to do." Stacy had helped to open and manage some restaurants in places like Hawaii. She was very good at marketing and advertising, organizing things and getting them going; I have a good sense and exciting ideas about product development. With our combination of skills we thought we'd do well opening up a really neat restaurant someday. That was our initial goal, until we realized we didn't have any money! We headed back to the drawing board...

Marriage of Theory and Practice

Joining together their passions for both practice and theory, this next couple are powerful facilitators of management conversations that provide the groundwork for their growth and the success of their students and clients.

LAURIE AND JEFFREY FORD

Laurie (65) and Jeffrey (62) Ford are a co-professional, copreneurial couple residing in Columbus, Ohio. She is a management consultant with a doctorate and he is a professor in the College of Business at Ohio State University. They met and fell in love in 1987 at a professional conference where Jeffrey was speaking on organizational transformation. By the end of the talk, Laurie knew she wanted to work with him for the rest of her life. They married two years later and have been married for 21 years. They are committed to making the concepts of management accessible to MBA students and clients alike. Their mission is to upgrade management conversations.

Laurie: It's a good marriage of theory and practice. I'd been a practicing consultant for a long time when Jeffrey introduced me to some people here in Columbus, and I started doing consulting here. There was a time when I was incorporated and Jeffrey handled all the financial matters. Now we're doing business together more and more. Jeffrey's doing the website. We write products together. He knows all the literature. We write books or special reports, and he puts them out on the website. We have a newsletter with more than 10,000 subscribers at this point. Who knew that people were so interested in management?

Knowledge and Respect

As you deepen your respect for each other and expand your knowledge of how you work together in business, your satisfaction grows. Respect for each other's talents and strengths allows **Claudette and Ade Faison**, who you read about earlier [p. 31] to continue developing a thriving human services business.

Claudette: My natural way of being is the driver. I think it can be a strength and a weakness, but for the most part it's an asset that I'm the one saying, "Let's go, we've got to get there!" But every driver needs to know that someone is saying, "You can do it!" And that's what Ade does. I drive and he says, "Yeah." And then when he wants to drive, I don't like it!

In terms of what Ade brings to the relationship — among other things it is consistency. He's the one who knows the beginning, the middle and the end of what happened. He keeps track of the goal and what it is going to take to get us there. I can count on him to be consistent in the partnership.

Trust and the Freedom to Disagree

In relationship and in business, differences can drive us apart or fuel our next venture. Dissimilarities can offer the opportunity to discuss and wrestle with difficult feelings and choices in order to arrive at a deeper understanding of the issues. The outcome can be the drafting of an even better vision or plan, or a change in roles or priorities. It is essential to have the ability and courage to discuss things openly and negotiate fairly.

Trusting each other's skills, even in the midst of disagreements or difficult conversations, is an essential ingredient for accomplishment. Trusting in your own strengths and those of your partner is built over time, and comes from knowing each other and working together. Trust and friendship is the heart of the matter discussed in the next story.

JUDY ROSENBERG AND ELIOT WINOGRAD

Judy Rosenberg (63) and Eliot Winograd (64) are the co-owners of Rosie's Bakery, a well known retail bakery with stores in the Boston area. Judy started the business from home in 1974 and moved to their premier location in Inman Square, Cambridge in 1978, at which point Eliot joined her. Together since 1976, they married in 1980 and divorced two years later but remain successful business partners and best friends. Judy and Eliot have the freedom to disagree about boundaries and roles because, ultimately, they trust each other.

Judy: Eliot is better at setting boundaries for himself. He would rather focus on work at work … that's it. When he leaves for work he wants his mind clear. For me, between my work and my kids, everything in my life is one big mush. I envy his ability to set his boundaries.

Eliot: I don't want to hear from Rosie's on Sunday. That is the one day I want to myself and my family, whatever I do or don't do. I don't want to be bothered by business on that day; that's how I feel.

Eliot: In terms of how we define our roles, people see us differently. If there is any operational problem, they will come to me. If someone in the kitchen has a question about recipe development, they would not come to me.

Judy: They probably look at me as the softie and him as the tough guy. I am not going to hold them accountable unless….

Eliot: It's got to be a real transgression. We play the roles of the good mother vs. the bad father. I get to be the disciplinarian. Judy has a great sense of aesthetics and how the products should taste. Employees open up to Judy a lot, which can be good and not good. People know that Judy has a good soul.

Judy: Eliot is organized and has great administrative skills. When he entered the business in 1978, it was in the red. He brings prices into line with what is realistic. He is more of an authoritarian figure, and that is also fruitful. I think people like me a lot, but I don't have the ability to confront them and keep things in line and balanced, which Eliot easily oversees and makes sure of. We don't really tread on each other's territory much. Sometimes there is conflict over a particular thing, and sometimes I will think he is being too hard about something.

Basically, we trust that the other is a good human being and that we will each always try to do the right thing. At times he will convince me that the best way to go is something other than what I think it is. We always agree that we would never choose to do something that lacks integrity. He might say that we can't do x for this person right now because of y, and I'll see his point. Eliot will think about issues and how things fit together for us as a company that keeps the overall context in mind.

Judy: Sometimes I have challenges with Eliot's style. I might think his style is too abrupt or insensitive. Usually, if that happens, I'll talk to him about it. He might get upset about something and have a knee jerk response and not deal with it in what I think is a professional way. Sometimes he'll disagree and other times he'll say I'm right, that he should have kept himself in abeyance.

Eliot: People will talk with Judy. They know to go to Judy. I only have one child and he finds it easier to go to his mother. Using that analogy, people sort of know how to play Judy a little. They come to her and Judy will come advocating to me and perhaps not see the whole picture, how everything plays together. Sometimes that has created difficulties for us when she focuses on only that one person and wants to make it okay for them.

Judy: Eliot thinks I am disorganized — it comes with being creative!

Eliot: But with six stores you have to have systems.

Judy: I'll feel an urgency: for example, it's November, and we still have summer drinks. I don't care about the chaos; just take out the drinks for that season! It will be chaotic, but we'll have hot drinks. He'll say we have to roll them out systematically. It's the battle between the hard core facts and whatever it takes to grab the public. I am not convinced that the systems can't be broken for a short period of time to shake something up in the business. If you just stick with the systems, sometimes you will lose business. So maybe you'll lose $10 on the hot drinks today, but at least you'll have them.

Division of Labor

If you have been struggling with conflicting points of view, remember that they can be fertile ground for learning about yourself and your partner. The differences can guide you to divide tasks so that each partner has the freedom to contribute in what they do best. **Nick and Mitra Lore**, who successfully run Rockport Institute, their career coaching company, [p. 25] describe the balance they have achieved in working together on a business that Nick started and Mitra joined.

Nick: Over the years, Mitra has grown into working on it, and there have been positive and negative aspects to that. Mitra provides a lot of support and is a source of energy that moves things forward. She's the executive management for planning and decision making. But I do most of the actual work.

Mitra: I take care of the big picture and I keep it very alive. When Nick is in the trenches working with clients, I have a chance to step back and keep looking and say, "What is missing now?" I love seeing the vision and technology of Rockport becoming part of the school system. That's where the juice is for me. People who are committed to picking a career that fits them perfectly know we are here with a master plan for them to use.

College Sweethearts Playing in Different Domains

Knowing each other from early adulthood can be an advantage in starting a business later in life. As you mature together, you have the opportunity to clarify and revise your life and business goals.

This couple met in college and have had a long time to distinguish their strengths and differences before they went into business together.

RICHARD TUBMAN AND PEGGY BURNS

Peggy Burns (57) and Richard Tubman (58) started out selling electronic games in a computer store that Richard began as a Harvard Business School graduate who was eager to own a business. They sold it in 1984 and eventually entered a furniture business that Richard's grandfather had founded. With one of Richard's brothers, they expanded Circle Furniture into five successful stores in the greater Boston area. College sweethearts, they have been married for thirty-two years and are the parents of two grown children, Erica (29) and Max (25).

Richard: We had a computer business that was born for one reason — I needed a computer. The worst thing in my family is to buy something retail. I couldn't buy one, so I had to start a store.

In our furniture business, we've been able to work well together because we have different domains. It would be much more of a challenge if we were doing the same thing. I am more focused on the arithmetic, the back office stuff; Peggy is focused on the front of the store. I have no taste and no affinity for fabrics, while she is great at organization, color, whimsy and playfulness.

Peggy: Richard is tech support for the whole company. We refer to him as "Daddy Google." [Laughter]

Richard: The children call me that, too — they call me in the middle of the night on their cell phones and assume I know the answer to all technical questions.

Argue, Take Risks and Thrive on the Challenges

How many of us get stuck and derailed from our intention or purpose when we cannot honestly and directly express our needs to our partners? Being able to argue, take risks and thrive on challenges enriches a relationship and is a great model for students and clients, as we see in this story. **Laurie and Jeffrey Ford,** who have separate careers but are increasingly working together, [p. 38] openly share their own set of agreements and arguments that serve their business.

Laurie: Looking at the question of how those challenges impacted us in our relationship and in business, we have funny arguments about this. We can actually have a heated argument about strategic planning and what it means and what its role is in a corporation.

Jeffrey: We don't argue a lot about what most people talk about, like where are we going for dinner, who's going to cook, or how are we going to decorate. It all seems to be around strategic management.

Laurie: Jeffrey is mostly working with people who are studying management consulting, but then I, as a management consultant, am taking them out into the world and seeing what really rings true as they manage in actual businesses. What lands for people? What makes sense for people? Sometimes we give ourselves a lot of permission to have a great big fight about strategic planning, which lasts maybe fifteen minutes. But always new things come out of it. None of these challenges have negatively impacted our relationship.

Jeffrey: My experience of the challenges is that they pretty much keep us going and growing. Laurie will bring back something new from work. Almost everything we deal with is work — I will look at it, and I might talk to a colleague. I have to grow into it, find out what it is.

Laurie: It's discovery all the time.

Jeffrey: I can't think of any area of challenge that's walled off or forbidden.

Roles

The roles we learned in our nuclear and extended families and continue in our work lives may or may not serve us. In creating or expanding a business, we have the opportunity to consciously design roles that provide the clarity and flexibility to succeed in business and take care of our families in the best way possible.

In both heterosexual and homosexual couples, issues of gender roles and equality surface. It has been inspiring for us to hear so many stories from women and men who have gone far beyond gender stereotypes to deal with these issues. For the sake of the family and the business, they have done what needed to be done without any question about what was considered socially appropriate to their gender. Women have spoken about experiencing their public power and influence, and men have talked about deepening their personal capacities for nurturing the family. These couples are thoughtful collaborators who enjoy the benefits of their applied wisdom.

Communication, Collaboration and Change

The experience of true collaboration with a partner can be deeply satisfying. When we are able to bring the best of ourselves to the relationship, our hearts sing and our businesses thrive. This couple tells a simple story of collaboration where they demonstrated consciousness, flexibility and clarity about roles.

RON AND ALINA CHAND

Alina (55) and Ron (68) Chand have been married for 31 years, raised three kids, and been in business together for 23 years. They have bought and sold four businesses, among them Shenango Advanced Ceramics LLC, where Alina served as CEO. Ron also served as a Senior R&D Staff Member at Oak Ridge National Laboratory. Together they own and operate Chand Associates, Inc., an advanced ceramics and porous metal products business based in Massachusetts.

Ron: We worked together, we learned from each other and, of course, I'm still learning all the time from Alina. I would not send out a letter, in all honesty, that she has not read, because the way I construct sentences, the meaning could be construed incorrectly. I always rely on her opinion.

Alina: I have never put any burdens on Ron where I said, "You have to be home at five, that's the supper time, that's when the kids and I are having supper." It was more like, "This is the time the kids and I are going to have supper. If you can make it, fine; if you're not here, we'll eat and I'll put a plate aside for you later."

Now, of course, when I got more involved in the business, when I became the president and I had to go out to dinner with customers, then Ron would be home at a regular time and take over all the functions with the kids. So it worked well.

Dreams, Sorrow and Miracles: Raising Two "Babies"

The experience of loss and sorrow can stop us or propel us forward. In moving ahead, it can engage the strengths of bravery, resiliency and flexibility. **Anne and Christopher Ellinger** [p. 19], are a courageous couple who experienced the miracle and collaborative challenge of raising two "babies" at the same time — a child and a business.

Christopher: In the early years of our relationship, we were both insecure about work. We had big dreams but not much practical experience. Anne was especially afraid that if she settled down with me, she'd stay confused about work forever because I was just as confused as she. Fast forward nine years together: Anne is finally sure she wants to have a child together, but what I want is to work together. I'm afraid of losing our world-changing dreams, and our lives becoming solely absorbed into childrearing, as I've seen happen for so many others. So we "cut a deal." I agree to having a child, and Anne promises that within five years we'll do some kind of work out in the world together — not necessarily our main paid work, but something of significance to us both.

Of course, they say God laughs when people make plans. First, we get pregnant immediately! Then, our daughter Kaia mysteriously dies just before birth, which catapults our lives into a different trajectory than our carefully laid five-year plan. Three months after Kaia's death, we take a work trip to England. We have such a wonderful time working together, we say, "Let's go for it!" On that trip, we conceive both our son Micah, and the business that becomes *More Than Money*.

Many times we've said it's been like raising twins to have both "babies" at the same time. It's probably been hard at times for our son, having an invisible sibling who sucks up a lot of his parents' creative energy. But he's also had the benefit of seeing his parents working together doing what they love.

Anne: For six years Christopher had been working on writing a book called "We Gave Away a Fortune." He was struggling with a terrible writing block and over years I said dozens of times, "Would you forget that book? It's killing you!" This, of course, would only make him more determined to continue it.

Well, I love writing, and I joined as his work partner right as the book was about to go to the publisher. Neither of us was satisfied with the quality of the writing, so we negotiated with the publisher for more time. We spent the last month of my pregnancy working 16 hours a day completely rewriting the book, making it clear and tight and vivid. It was just what the doctor ordered! It completely took our minds off obsessing about whether this second baby would live. He did just fine — our son Micah is now 19, taller than both of us and pursuing his passion for acrobatics.

In hindsight, it feels like a miracle that we wrote the book at all. Its publication was instrumental to More Than Money's launch. More Than Money was a vital steppingstone towards Bolder Giving, which has had an impact beyond our wildest dreams. This is the way life happens. We couldn't have planned any of those events, yet they were key to our life and our business.

Flexibility and Confidence in Gender Roles

Multiple projects and multiple children — how do some people do it all? When you are in the midst of struggling with your own complex situation, you somehow find solutions to seemingly impossible problems. This is especially possible when you have open and flexible gender roles in your family. What this couple has done and continue doing seems unusual — if not impossible. Their confidence in themselves and their communities comes through and is a tremendous support in their life and work.

ALLEN AND THERESA DAYTNER

Allen (48) and Theresa (43) Daytner have been a couple for 17 years and married for 13. They met working together for a large general contractor in the Washington, DC area. Residents of Maryland, they have been copreneurs for almost five years. Theresa had two businesses before they started the Daytner Construction Group, based in Maryland, which functions as the project and construction manager for anyone, large or small, who wants to build, including owners, developers, universities, etc. A creative twosome who love to travel and explore, the Daytners also managed the development of a whitewater rafting company. "We have positioned ourselves so we can do it all." They are parents of seven children — "yours, mine and ours" — ranging in age from 21 to 6-year-old twins.

Theresa: We are independent, confident people. We both feel exactly the same way. We don't need our kids to look to us as the only adults in their lives. I had a great time when I went to Idaho for a month. Everyone was happy.

Allen: She'll go to Idaho and I'll go to my college reunion. My friends think something is wrong. How can you as a man take care of all these kids? We don't have defined roles. We are both parents and can each take care of our kids. We have so many kids — you take some, I take some.

Theresa: Whatever needs to be done, someone does it. We are interchangeable.

Allen: I do the cooking and grocery shopping. This doesn't seem unusual to us.

Theresa: The running joke is about all the things I don't do!

Allen: We both take time off and emphasize the importance of the flexibility we give to our family. I know I value my friendships. I have the greatest friends and they have been the same for thirty years. There has been no reason to change. My friends can count on me. With my commitments to family and business, I don't have a lot of time to forge new relationships.

Having one career for life is no longer the norm as it was for past generations. Moving away from the security of working for one company for your entire adult life opens the door to creativity. A couple's flexibility can enable both of them to succeed and enjoy the process immensely, rather than getting caught up in endless negotiations about roles and logistics.

If a couple is lucky enough to grow up, so to speak, inside of their relationship, switching roles can become second nature instead of a struggle. When one person goes to school to get a degree, the other takes care of the bills. When one person goes to work, the other puts the children to bed. To them, it's not an amazing or unusual choice to participate fully and equally in pursuing a career or raising a family. They spend less energy bridging different worlds and can more easily find a way to share power that supports the relationship rather than allowing it to threaten their roles or territory.

Dividing Time and Tasks for Talent and Leadership

The next two stories illustrate division of responsibilities in a way that supports the leader and the partner in both circumstances. Each of the original business owners needed the particular skills of their partner, and brought them in as the business was ready to grow.

DAVID NICHOLAS AND DAVID MIRANOWICZ

How many people do you know who have created a makeup training center? This original idea was developed by David Nicholas (52). He and David Miranowicz (43) are the owners of David Nicholas International, Inc. and DNI Cosmetics. They run the only makeup training center on the East Coast licensed by a state Board of Cosmetology. David Nicholas is a makeup artist who graduated from aesthetics school; David Miranowicz is a trained businessman who supports his partner's creativity. One impressive application of their work, both locally and internationally, is contributing their time and skill in reconstructive makeup to help children and adults recover with dignity from disfiguring burn traumas or war injuries. Residents of Boston's North Shore, they have known each other for 18 years, been together for 16, and married for seven.

David N.: I've done everything old school — cut and paste. I have three web sites and I don't even know how to plug the computer in. He does all the scheduling with his iPhone, and he takes care of that aspect of the business, which is so important today. You almost can't run a business without all this technology behind you, and I'm just not a technical person. Fortunately, David is. And because of his experience in modeling and fashion, he also knows my industry. The two of us really work well together to make it all happen.

David M.: While I graduated from Merrimack College in Business Administration, I've learned more about how to run a business by working with David compared to what I learned in school. The technical, financial and organizational needs of the business demand that I be very practical and flexible in ways I learned on the job, not from the books.

Right Place, Right Time

This next couple was at the right place at the right time. They were able to respond to a new way of doing business that supported their niche market.

LIZA AND BLU ATWOOD

Based on the length of time spent together in business, Liza Roeser Atwood (41) and Blu Atwood (39) are among the newest entrepreneurs we interviewed. In fact, the day of our interview was their first official day as copreneurs. Liza has been an entrepreneur since 1996 and initially started each of their two businesses. They have been married for six years, live in Ojai, California and are the parents of two young daughters, Alexandra (5) and Eloise (1).

Liza: We have two businesses. Farm Fresh Exports is a business to business enterprise that wholesales flowers to large retailers throughout the world. Our main markets are the U.S., Guam, Russia, Italy and Kuwait. Our flower farms are mainly in Ecuador, but two years ago we started to expand into Colombia, New Zealand and California, and soon we are going to open up Costa Rica. We don't house or have an inventory of product. Flowers go directly from the farm to the wholesaler.

Fiftyflowers.com is a Web site for the consumer. We sell bulk flowers or do-it-yourself flowers for weddings. Our niche market is brides on a budget. The flowers go from farm to doorstep by FedEx service.

Blu: Today is my first official day as Chief of Marketing, Finance and Operations! I will be developing business partnerships, heading up search engine marketing and generating offline TV and radio coverage. I had a day job with an Internet startup company for the three years since Liza and I met, and a night job helping Liza along the way. Now I am full time with Liza and together we drive what we think of as a family business. Marketing and technology are my areas of specialization.

Liza: I am President and Founder. I handle public relations. I am ultimately responsible for finances and operations. I used to dabble in marketing, but I am no comparison to Blu in this area. I was a Peace Corps volunteer in Ecuador, and although I am 100% North American, my heart is Ecuadorian.

When I finished my assignment, I realized that I didn't want to go back to the States. Living in Ecuador for twelve years, I learned that Ecuador has the most amazing roses in the world because of the perfect climate, and there weren't many people to sell the flowers. I was hired into the flower business as a bicultural and bilingual VP of marketing for a very large corporation. One day I decided that I was tired of doing all the work for someone else. My clients said they would come with me; that's when I formed Farm Fresh Exports and began to develop a reputation in the industry.

UPS approached me in 2000 and expressed an interest in going directly from the farm to the consumers. Flower exports were new. It was unheard of to bypass the Miami importers and bring in flowers from the farmer to the wholesale house and to the florist. UPS encouraged me to do just that and accepted my application. There I was, in a third world country with the Internet, and I could build a Web site with the help of a great designer friend in Michigan. That's how I got started.

Role Change for Dad and Stepmom, Too

A couple can contemplate a change in roles over years or it can happen very quickly. Either way, there are adjustments to be made for each individual, for the couple, the family and the business.

Changing roles have opened up new possibilities for **Jeffrey and Sandy Davis** [p.12] as they continue to enjoy successful businesses and more vacations. We've seen enormous role flexibility in most of the couples we've interviewed.

Jeffrey: It's amazing how quickly it changed for us. I was working about 80 hours a week at Mage LLC and still picking up the kids three days a week. I picked them up early and they learned how to adapt to my schedule. I never missed a pick up date; I didn't cancel for business events and I didn't travel for business. I structured my career so that the kids didn't lose out on parenting. I made the choice to build a local practice for that reason. I've had clients say to me, "If you can't be here, I can't work with you." And I've said, "I am sorry; I am a father and my priority is to take care of my kids." For four years I did every bit of shopping, every bit of laundry, the entire pick up for the kids, all the cooking. As soon as Sandy sold Pioneer, I looked at her and said, "OK, It's enough, you've got to come back."

Sandy: It was automatic. I wanted to be back. Because of Jeffrey's parenting style, I don't know if I could have done what I did with Pioneer if I had taken as active a role in picking up the kids and cooking the meals. I enjoyed helping when I could, but now that the business has been sold, I'm much more active and I've taken on a lot of what he was doing then. One of the reasons I fell in love with Jeffrey was that he was such a dedicated parent. He reminded me of my father — no matter how hard he worked he was a phenomenal parent. However, Jeffrey outdoes everyone I've ever seen.

When he was picking up the kids, he stopped work at 4:00 and didn't schedule anything after that. Whenever the kids had a school vacation, Jeffrey would take them away somewhere. I learned that either I could go with them or not see them. That changed my life. I hadn't really ever taken any substantial vacation time and now I do and I love it. We used to go on exotic vacations, but then we bought a house on Cape Cod. Now we really enjoy spending most of our vacation time either on the Cape or at our family home in Florida, often with our children, Rachel (15) and Michael (23).

Business Success, Marriage Failure

People ask: What if the marriage doesn't last, what will happen to the business? Or what if the business fails, will the marriage fail too? Combining a personal relationship and a business relationship seems too risky to many. Others take the leap and work with what happens over time. If people are honest about the parts of the relationship that don't work, the parts that do work still have the possibility of flourishing when both business partners have a clear intention to make it so.

For **Mark Andrus and Stacy Madison** [p. 36], being flexible about their roles meant ending their marriage while still remaining strong business partners. We asked if there was a relationship between the marriage, getting divorced and developments in the business, and if they had different goals.

Stacy: We were better as friends than we were as a married couple.

Mark: Of course, there was an attraction, but we started off as friends and all of a sudden we were working together with the same goals, the same passions.

Stacy: We were 30, and in the beginning we loved each other.

Mark: Our friends were getting married and we thought why not? We spend all this time together, we're headed in the same direction, let's get married. Once that happened, it changed the relationship and we weren't as comfortable in that type of relationship. We were better being friends and business partners. At the time we went to marriage counseling because we knew we were probably going to separate and we were able to begin that process before resentments set in. I think people miss the boat when they stay in a relationship past where it's supposed to end and then they get resentful.

Stacy: We might not have had a successful marriage but we like to say we had a successful divorce.

Mark: A successful friendship.

Stacy: A successful divorce.

Mark: A successful business relationship.

Stacy: Friendship, divorce and business relationship… you know, that's not so bad. We got three good ones there.

Boundaries

We all have boundaries, whether or not we are aware of them at any given moment. We usually experience our limits when someone steps over them. Boundaries can be set to serve us so that our personal space is respected and we can enjoy our relationship and be productive in our business. It is important to identify our limitations at a given time or in a particular situation, and to clearly communicate them to those who can help us get what we need. This will allow for healthier communication.

Clear Boundaries Between Work and Home

It is challenging for many business couples to set clear parameters for their business conversations. The compelling nature of these conversations often trumps the need for a break and a chance to focus on matters like self care, the relationship or the family. Choosing powerfully to make the shift takes intention and discipline. This next couple uses their spiritual practices to support them.

Claudette and Ade Faison [p. 31] shared their contrasting views about creating boundaries between work and personal conversations between the boardroom and the bedroom.

Ade: You know we've attempted to do just that — to finish work before we get home. We ask, "How was your day, how did your day go?" Then when we get home early enough, we can enjoy just cooking together.

Claudette: There aren't any boundaries. You're making that up.

Ade: No, I'm not making it up. I'm aware of it. I'm aware that there are times when I do not want to have conversations about work in the bedroom.

Claudette: I never want to have a conversation about work in the bedroom.

Ade: But often they show up.

Claudette: We have not successfully created boundaries so that work discussions don't come up in the bedroom.

Ade: Sometimes we do, but from doing spiritual work together, we have gotten a lot better sense of how to set boundaries.

Marrying Different Styles

There are unusual instances where one partner in the couple sets boundaries between home and work and the other does not. **Sherri and Terry McArdle** [p. 29] have found a way to honor both their preferences and their relationship.

Terry: Sherri's life and business are almost inseparable. If Sherri is not thinking about the family and our two children (ages 27 and 18), she is thinking about the business. Am I as binary as that? The bulk of what we talk about is family and business, yet I've got this whole other component. My life is very different outside of work. I am focused on spiritual life and my community of friends. I've spent a lot of time learning, and I've been active in my synagogue since I converted in 2000. I was on the board of trustees, the executive board, and I taught history there. I also have many friends and spend a lot of time with buddies playing bimonthly poker games and a lot of golf. At this point we are enjoying life. My approach is probably more traditional than Sherri's. She loves her work and works her love.

Commitment is a powerful force. The famous "commitment" quote, written by the Scottish mountaineer W.H. Murray, is relevant here:

Until one is committed, there is hesitancy, the chance to draw back, always ineffectiveness. Concerning all acts of initiative (and creation), there is one elementary truth the ignorance of which kills countless ideas and splendid plans: that the moment one definitely commits oneself, then providence moves too. A whole stream of events issues from the decision, raising in one's favor all manner of unforeseen incidents, meetings

and material assistance, which no man could have dreamt would have come his way. I learned a deep respect for one of Goethe's couplets:
  "Whatever you can do or dream you can, begin it.
  Boldness has genius, power and magic in it. Begin it now." [2]

When we commit, the impossible becomes possible. All sorts of things occur to help one that would never otherwise have occurred. Commitment calls forth the energy to vitalize an entrepreneurial couple into taking the action required to succeed.

Our Perspective on Commitment

Commitment is an active engagement — without action there is no creation or growth. Sandy and Lon Golnick, who you will meet shortly, define commitment as action in favor of your values. Once you are committed with your resources you have begun to open new relationship and business possibilities. In this chapter we have named and explored the personal strengths, skills and resources that you must tap into in order to launch and develop your business. Here are some conversations to explore before we move to the next chapter, which is about the role of family in generating and sustaining your business.

Chapter Takeways

1. Identify your strengths and differences and those of your partner; then trade notes to see how similar or different your analyses are.

2. Talk with your partner about how your roles and boundaries are working for you in the business and in the relationship.

3. Where do your roles and boundaries either enhance or hinder the business and the relationship?

4. Have a dialogue with your partner about one change you could initiate in each area that would ensure greater success or satisfaction in your personal and business life.

---

[2] This whole quote is most often attributed to Goethe, but it is actually near the beginning of Murray's *The Scottish Himalayan Expedition* (1951). The ending couplet is the only part from Goethe in a very loose translation from *Faust* by John Anster in 1835.

Thoughts on this Chapter

_____

_____

_____

_____

_____

_____

_____

_____

_____

_____

_____

_____

_____

_____

_____

_____

_____

_____

_____

_____

_____

"If I have made any valuable discoveries, it has been owing more to patient attention than to any other talent."

—SIR ISAAC NEWTON (1642–1727)
BRITISH SCIENTIST

CHAPTER THREE

SUCCESSFULLY "INCORPORATING" YOUR CHILDREN AND EXTENDED FAMILY

T HE DEMANDS THAT A BUSINESS places on a couple can challenge even the strongest relationship. Entrepreneurial couples must be proactive in attending to the needs of the relationship and of each partner. They are constantly learning from their experience and refining their skills. They are willing to act, evaluate and readjust as they learn what works for their relationship and their business.

When we begin to take family into account, these issues are amplified. The more people there are in the system, the more responsive couples need to be to the shifts and changes brought about by the evolving needs of the family.

This chapter explores the intersection between family and business; the inspiration and motivation of family, the positive influences of extended family, and the benefits for children and extended family members of couples choosing to be in business together. Equally important are the challenges of integrating work and family, and the sources of support that need to be in place for it all to work.

Family can play a large role in motivating or inspiring couples to start a business. The business certainly influences the family, especially if there are children, and the children also influence the business. Couples in business together need flexibility to make the daily challenges work, and if they are parents, success means learning how to deal with being parents, caregivers and entrepreneurs all at the same time. In other words, they must become expert jugglers! This is a challenge and also a benefit: the desire for greater control and freedom in personal and family relationships was part of what led many couples to create businesses.

How family and business interact is the key to the success of each. In this chapter we hear from couples who have important insights and stories about this interaction. The conversations cover family as inspiration, the impact of children and the role of extended family.

Part One: Inspiration

Many of the couples we interviewed identified their children as a major source of inspiration and motivation. Others looked toward their parents, grandparents or other family members for inspiration and guidance. The wide variety of experiences makes this discussion a rich one.

A Business That's All About Family

While a family-based business is not a career direction that suits everyone, it can be a less common opportunity to experience harmony between work and home, which can offer deep satisfaction and joy.

SANDY AND LON GOLNICK

Sandy (68) and Lon (70) Golnick have been married for 47 years. They have two grown children and six grandchildren. They moved from San Francisco to San Diego when it became clear that their daughters had chosen to settle there. Formerly educators, Lon and Sandy have highly developed skills from their years of experience teaching and coaching families. They have integrated their unique perspective on family into the very fabric of the business they co-created and co-run: Relationship & Families ByDesign.

Lon: We begin and end with family. If you ask people what family means to them, they will come up with some version of "everything." But if you watch the way we live as a culture, you'll see that we take family for granted. Sandy and I are actively engaged in the practice of putting our family, our children and grandchildren, first. We live what we advocate in our practice. Our way of being in life has shifted from making it in life to supporting what is most important in our lives.

Sandy: One of the great things about our work is that our children are often included in whatever ways work for them. Our children are our teachers and partners as well.

Lon: Families give you what you fundamentally value. They launch you into life and give you what you carry with you whether you like it or not. We believe if we can make a difference in families, we can make a difference in the world.

Sandy: Families are life defining — that is the nature of family.

Lon: We identified three things that we are interested in for the remainder of our lives: family, work and adventures together. Then we began to see that family is a network of relationships, and also explored how we could work with specific relationships to affect the whole family.

Sandy: Our work is an exploration into our default way of relating to others. Our definition of commitment is having values and acting on them.

Lon: We have taken on the job of illuminating the fundamental design of relationships. However, it's clear that many people don't live that way. Once we identify the concerns, problems and disappointments that people often experience over time, we can think of familial relationships in a new way and be in touch with their natural aspects. In our experience, people don't need more instructions about what to do; they need to know they have the freedom to create.

Original Family as Inspiration

There are many sources of inspiration and motivation for a couple in business. Dr. Wayne Dyer, in his public television presentation on "*The Power of Intention*," distinguishes motivation from inspiration. He describes motivation as something that comes from outside of us and demands that we take action. In contrast, inspiration is an internal experience of an energy that flows through us and invites us to be creative and expansive.

We discussed motivation and inspiration in depth in Chapter One. An important thing to know about inspiration is that it breathes life into our motivation and allows us to keep our mojo working for the long haul.

Following in Their Footsteps

The stories from the lives of our parents and grandparents and the memories we hold of living with family provide solid ground to stand upon when couples are inspired to create businesses of their own. The next two stories describe inspiration that comes from our parents' generation.

Laurie and Jeffrey Ford [p. 38] recount how they picked up the mantle of their parents' values.

Jeffrey: I'm clearly my parents' son. I definitely carry the mark of what they considered to be appropriate, right and good.

Laurie: The main contributions from my family background were twofold: my mother held a strong conviction that you need to contribute; my dad introduced us to Unitarian Universalism because he wanted me to think. Instead of having better answers he wanted me to ask better questions.

I did not grow up in a business environment. Neither of my parents were college graduates, but my mom did go back to get her college degree when she was in her fifties. My dad was a Renaissance man— an intellectual, a sculptor, an artist, a writer— and he earned his living as a graphic artist and copywriter. I think he helped me discover that I wanted to work for myself. I worked for other people but found it too limiting; I very much enjoy being able to carve out my own path.

Jeffrey: My beliefs and expectations around money come from being part of the professional working class: you've got to earn it, it's not just going to be handed to you. Whatever you acquire is your own acquisition. Power and influence don't come from an inheritance; it's not a given.

Laurie: I've got the same kind of belief: you have to work for it. The greatest source of power and influence that I'm acquainted with in my life is education. I grew up with books, reading and the importance of education. I'm aware that when I do my work I'm educating people and giving them some power.

The entrepreneurial backgrounds of **Wendy Capland and Chris Michaud** [p. 14] have served them well. They were both directly mentored by their fathers and came from long business heritages.

Chris: I come from a family of entrepreneurs that spans 400 years. My family members are mostly carpenters and contractors. I was one of the first men to break away from that in my family because I just didn't get the sticks and the geometry. To me it was all hard work, cold and no fun building houses in Maine. So it's interesting that I wound up in the real estate business. My father is in his seventies and still building houses.

Two of my brothers are builders, and one prefers carpentry work. My sister is in the pet grooming business. At age 18 or 19, I had set a goal to be in business by the time I was 30. I was 29 years and ten months old when I opened up my first real estate company. By the time I was 38 years old, I had become a millionaire. Then I got a divorce and I didn't have a million dollars anymore. I can tell you that a million dollars doesn't mean that much.

Part Two: Our Children

As we delve into the following sections on benefits for children and challenges for the family, we invite you to examine how these issues have occurred in your own personal and business lives: where you succeeded and where you got stuck, the benefits received and the challenges met.

How Copreneurship Helps Children Learn and Grow

Being in business as a couple can benefit the family in diverse ways. It:

- Inspires children when they see their parents successfully engaged in work they love;

- Provides built-in training about setting boundaries and balancing personal and collective needs;

- Gives children the opportunity to participate in the business as appropriate for their own stages of growth; and

- Provides learning opportunities as they see parents create solutions for the stresses of conflicting business and family needs.

Some couples are adamant that their children not succeed them in the business. Others see their business as a gift to their children. Still others are neutral. Which perspective most accurately reflects your own?

Independent People with Independent Businesses

John Witty and Ellyn Spragins [p. 15] are a co-professional couple living in New Jersey whose commitment to parenting motivated them as they mapped out their professional paths. High school sweethearts who have been married for over 36 years, they see their business ventures as contributing to the independence of their two young adult children.

Ellyn: One reason I chose the route of a freelancer rather than an editor is that I wanted to be home and participate in my kids' lives rather than dip in and out of their daily activities. This was a big decision for me. I can remember our daughter feeling very frustrated in middle school about the fact that we were always home! I am curious to see what she thinks about that later.

Having a business will influence our kids in the messages we give them. We are planting the idea that they are independent people who can make up their own work. It's up to them to think and be creative. This is very much in line with their generation — how entrepreneurial they become and how many networks they will have to create markets for themselves.

John: My kids don't really know what I do. They know I am interested in money, stocks and the markets because we talk about it. I don't think what I do affects them particularly. They don't have an interest yet; they don't have an understanding of Wall Street or stocks or investments, and I don't expect them to. I think they are pleased that Ellyn and I provide nicely for them. Ellyn is an example of someone who has desired independence, in contrast to her Dad, who is the ultimate corporate kind of guy. But I think back to my father as a small town lawyer and grandfather and I see that none of us is oriented towards being a company kind of guy. We never meant to climb the corporate ladder or spend 15 to 20 years at a single company. I think that is reflected in my work history and it's definitely filtered through to our kids.

Informed and Outspoken Children

Children observe and absorb what we as parents do, even without our intending to teach them about our work. The benefits of this early learning can assist them as they move out on their own. The following couple reared informed and outspoken young women as they developed their various networking ventures.

JEFFREY STAMPS AND JESSICA LIPNACK

Jeffrey Stamps (66) and Jessica Lipnack (63) are entrepreneurs, authors, networkers and communicators as well as innovators and activists in the technology field. They have been married for over 39 years and in business together the entire time. They are the parents of two grown daughters.

Jeffrey: Our daughters would have a lot to say about our being in business together. I'll tell you, from a father's point of view, that by far the most important factor has been that we have almost always worked out of the house; at other times our offices were just a quarter mile down the street in one direction or the other. The kids were always around computers and our work and to some degree they hate it and still complain, so we cannot talk about work in front of them.

Jessica: On the other hand, a great quote comes from our older daughter who is working in a software company. A woman whom she had known for maybe six months asked her what her background was and what her parents did. When she explained, the other woman said, "Oh, my God, thank you! Now I understand why whenever a complicated business issue comes up, you know how to answer it." In fact, she was exposed to this kind of organizational thinking all her life.

Business Possibilities for the Next Generation
When parents step out, sometimes children are motivated to step in and help. Here is an inspiring account of a situation where necessity was the mother of invention and shaped the lifetime career choice of this couple's son.

JEAN AND HOWARD LE VAUX
Jean (80) and Howard (77) Le Vaux, residents of Cambridge, Massachusetts, are long-time business owners. They have been married for 45 years and are the parents of four children and the grandparents of five. Together they own Le Vaux Associates, Inc., and are well respected holistic real estate brokers. Committed to going "beyond the ordinary," they do whatever it takes to satisfy their customers in the transaction of buying or selling a house. As much as making the sale they are equally concerned with its impact on the client.

Jean: After eating one too many takeout meals or pizzas, Ari, our 11-year-old son, offered to take over the cooking. He learned to cook, and now as an adult he is a professional chef!

Modeling a Business Career
Clearly our experiences as business people can rub off on our children. In this next story, the children chose careers that followed the business models set by their parents, **Wendy Capland and Chris Michaud** [p. 14].

Wendy: My kids don't know me as a person working in a company. They grew up with me as an entrepreneur. They just think this is the way people work. My son declared himself a business major in his freshman year in college. Chris's son has definitely been influenced by his father's choices. He wants to follow in his father's footsteps in every way in life, including business. He started a business around the same age as his father did. When my daughter was in elementary school, she was shocked to find out that her friend's mother didn't come home until 5 pm. I was home when she got home from school most of the time. And if I wasn't here, Chris was. On the other hand, my children have influenced my life in that the business has been organized around their needs and schedules.

Chris: We've done all the estate planning for the next generation and beyond. Part of what I'm doing now is to make sure that the next generation has business ventures that they can take over.

The Love of Work

How inspiring would it be for you to wake each day exclaiming, "It doesn't get any better than this?" We all aspire to love our work and wish the same for our children. Some couples' joy in their work has profoundly influenced their growing children's points of view. The influence of the business on children can have both positive and negative aspects. It can show them how much fun you can have working, and at the same time they may worry that they won't be able to find work that *they* love as much as you love what *you* do.

On the other hand, it is an inspiration to see their parents creating a business that they love, something that goes beyond just making money for its own sake. This is especially important when children grow up in affluent settings and are focused mainly on themselves, because in those privileged circumstances they can often not understand or even disrespect the deeper social purpose behind their parent's work.

Creating a Vibrant Network of Support

Once owning a business and having children are a reality, we are faced with how to do it all. Some of us plan ahead, and others take action when confronted with more to do than there are hours, or challenged to be effective both as entrepreneurs and as parents. We reach out for help from our families, friends and communities. We often find caretakers to help who then become extended family.

Committed to Plans for Success

With two children to rear and two businesses to grow, **Richard Rosen and Marguerite Piret** [p. 22] became very focused on making plans and taking actions that would allow them to do their best. Normally, parents must make outside arrangements with family and non-family caretakers for at least part of the time. From the beginning this couple was committed to being highly successful, both in their respective businesses and as parents.

Richard: I was involved with both of my children while they were growing up, even though I was running a major international business. I was traveling a lot — going everywhere — and part of the time I was living in Houston, Texas. It was a tumultuous time. Marguerite, too, was busy with her business in Boston. The thing that is important is that we were committed to our children most of all. We spent a lot of money and built an addition to our house, which is essentially a whole separate house, in order to be able to recruit a competent couple to live in our house and take care of the children and the household.

Marguerite: For us this meant making a huge financial commitment but it was our priority. We have had a married couple living in our house ever since Andrew was nine months old. For his first ten years, we had a couple from Czechoslovakia whose sons were raised with our two children, and we are still in touch. It turned out that our children (now 37 and 30) have done very well and we are proud of them.

Finding a Village of Support

When your finances are limited and you are running a small family business while supporting both elderly parents and children, you are constantly negotiating business and family life. Many couples are challenged by these particular life circumstances. When their trials and tribulations stressed their children, this next couple turned to friends and found a village of support. With help, they all thrived. Now, many years later, their children have grown into happy and accomplished adults.

RON AND LESLIE ARSLANIAN

Ron (64) and Leslie Arslanian (62) have been married for forty years. They are the owners of General Optical, a popular retail eyewear store in Cambridge, Massachusetts that has been their business for 32 years. They are the parents of two adult children, David (34) and Jamie (27).

Leslie: We opened in Cambridge on a wing and a prayer. Ron and his father did all the renovations… they built everything. I thought we were going to get divorced in that first 11 years. We gave up two great jobs, never had a day off or a vacation and rarely saw our son. We were dealing with sick, aging parents and paying for a startup business.

Ron: When asked to think about what contributed to our resiliency I believe that once we get invested in something, especially emotionally, it's like having a child, so we are never going to give up. Leslie's parents struggled for years to build a successful small business. Once the decision is made that you are going to make it, you can't throw in the towel.

Leslie: In those early years if there was a crisis with the kids, clearly we addressed the kids — that's a no brainer. But in general the business had to come first, say, before vacations, because it was our livelihood. Our son and daughter used to joke that the business was the first child in the family.

Ron: Did we balance work and family? I don't think we did balance it. It was hard for our children. The realities of not being able to keep things in balance are the most difficult part of being a couple in business, especially in a mom-and-pop business like ours. Even after we were able to hire employees, we found that customers had come to expect that Leslie and I would be at the store all the time.

Leslie: It was harder for our daughter Jamie than for our son David because there were no grandparents who could cover for us. She would come home from school and expect us to close at 6:00 pm and be home for dinner 15 or 20 minutes later. Yet, often we weren't able to say to a customer who arrived at 5:45 pm that we had to leave to have dinner with our child.

Ron: Still, we have two wonderful children and a terrific relationship with them. Even at their age, they ask when we will be on vacation so that they can spend time with us. It's remarkable to us that David is getting an MBA and going into the business world.

Leslie: He could have chosen to take on our business and grow it, but he and Jamie have an understandably negative reaction to owning a mom-and-pop business. I thought our business would be so different from my parents' deli. They offered us their business and we turned it down. My parents worked long hours and I never saw them. My aunt raised us. And then four or five years later, General Optical opened and we found ourselves doing exactly what my parents had done.

Ron: In the beginning we definitely turned to our parents for support. Then our support became and remains our friends. We have a group of close friends who understand. One of our best friends also owns a small business he runs by himself, and he became a substitute parent for David and Jamie.

Leslie: Before Hillary Clinton ever coined the phrase "It takes a village," we had two couples and one single guy who reared our children with us. They are the reason that we are a successful family unit which actually extends to the nine of us.

Ron: And none of them, even though they're all married, had children.

Support Within and Outside the Relationship

All working parents face the challenge of making suitable childcare arrangements. The following two couples had young children. They speak about their different experiences with getting and providing the childcare support that they needed in order to care for both their children and their businesses.

This first couple was resourceful within their nuclear family system but were also their own best source of support.

MARK AND KATE FRIEDMAN

Mark (47) and Kate (43) Friedman were founders and owners of two separate businesses. Mark is a Doctor of Chiropractic and Kate, a law school graduate, owned and ran a party rental supplies company. At the time of our interview they had been married for 12 years, were the parents of two small children, and had been in business 10 and 7 years, respectively. At the time of this writing, Mark and Kate are no longer married. While Mark continues to run his business and support the family, Kate has sold her business and returned to her original vocation as a practicing attorney.

Kate: We pay for any sources of support that we can. We use daycare to the utmost.

Mark: Since it's just the two of us there is literally no support system for us other than ourselves.

Kate: We are the support for each other and I also support a lot of my friends when they have troubles.

Mark: It's all a question of time. The number one aspect is that with children you have limited time to remain at the office because you have to pick them up or drop them off. We purposely don't want to send the children to daycare every single day. Since I arrive home late at night, I want to spend some day time with them. Thursday morning I stay home and Friday afternoon I leave work early to pick them up at school.

Kate: I was raised by two working parents, and our children are aware of the fact that work is important. My son asked me if I had to go to work and if so, why? I explained the need to earn money for food and toys, so he understood that. He also likes to help. They definitely know that when we're on the phone or in a meeting they cannot interrupt — that business is important.

However, being co-professional entrepreneurs only worked when they were able to work in tandem. Without the support of a partner at home or family nearby to care for the children, Kate was no longer able to put in the hours necessary to sustain the business on her own.

Faced with the choice of either leaving her children in the care of others or having them "live at work" with minimal quality time together in either case, she determined that it simply wasn't a viable lifestyle, and elected to sell the business.

The next couple has a very different situation…

BARRY FRIEDMAN AND VALERIE GATES

Barry Friedman (47) and Valerie Gates (45) live in Wellesley, Massachusetts. They met in an elevator at Brown University when Valerie was a teenager and Barry was a pre-med student who worked in Valerie's father's lab. They have been a couple for 28 years, married for 23, and are the parents of Cameron (15) and Olivia (10). Valerie started the business and Barry joined her in 2002. Gates Studio is an award-winning design firm offering complete creative design solutions.

Valerie: We help businesses with their marketing and creative design needs, including websites, branding, print and logo design. We started working together about 9 years ago, mainly because of the kids. Barry had been running creative services departments for other companies, and I had been working at the corporate level for CBS. We both wanted to try working together to create a more balanced life.

Barry: We wanted to make our lifestyle more flexible, and we've been able to do that. We're able to be more present in our kids' lives — not only by having the time to volunteer to coach their soccer teams and help out at their schools, but also by exposing them to the effort it takes to run a business.

Valerie: We took a huge leap, and our vision is to continue this balance between children, family and household while running a very successful business. We wanted to travel with our children and be able to take time off when needed. So far that's worked out, and we're also running a business that's become more successful every year.

We thought, "Why be present only when they're gone?" We decided we wanted to be there when they were little rather than later on. We are taking our liberties now, for them. There will always be time for us later. We work five days a week. I work 10:00 to 5:00, and Barry does the pick-ups and drop-offs. So he works from 9:00 to 5:00, and then from 8:00 to midnight most nights.

Barry: But I'll take off an hour here and there to pick up the kids, and I'll spend a couple of hours with my son or daughter if either of them has a soccer game. Then I'll work late to catch up. We each try to keep a pretty steady, eight hour workday.

Valerie: And Barry does all the cooking. We don't eat out much, but we do have dinner by candlelight with our kids every night. That's really important to us. We sit down and ask them how school was, and they ask us what we were working on!

The phone starts ringing at 9:00 am and we choose not to answer it after 5:00 pm. We do take time off for any school events, so it averages out about 35-40 hours a week per person. We also take weeks off when our schedules allow, so actually over a year we try to be flexible with our vacations. As long as we meet our income goals, then we feel comfortable giving ourselves a week for a trip in the summer, for example.

Valerie: I work out three days a week. That keeps me together mentally and physically.

Barry: I have a good group of soccer buddies. I play soccer in an adult league every Sunday morning. We have a very good support network and the neighbors are great.

Valerie: Our neighborhood is quite unique in that a lot of us are entrepreneurs who work at home. We cover a broad spectrum, from advertising, design and illustration to psychology and the arts. On occasion we work together, exchange advice, give support and spend time together after work. Isn't that fabulous? Sometimes we work on projects together.

We live and work in a historic district made up of cottages which offer an affordable style of housing with historic flavor. It is within walking distance to our kids' schools and the center of town, so we don't use our cars that much. We have a vibrant neighborhood with people who are interested in a certain lifestyle and share "the small house" philosophy. It doesn't come from family as much as from the neighborhood.

There's an awareness of the environment, and making conscious choices about how you want to live your life. I wanted to start a business that would allow me to be around for my children, and not be caught up in overworking to pay for all the trappings of success. I wanted to enjoy my kids before they left home.

Barry: We're very lucky. By being engaged in the neighborhood, we're more involved in the community and, as a result, we've also been able to build an awareness of our business and what we do for a living. On the other hand, advances in technology and the internet allow us to collaborate effectively with our out-of-town clients as well. It's remarkable when you think about it.

Valerie: There are many sleepless nights, even after ten years in business. It hasn't been an easy choice. The issue of affordable health care is one of the hardest things that we have had to deal with. Sometimes it's still a struggle, but we persevere because we really do believe in this way of life.

Integrating Work and Family Life
Whether our children enter our businesses or go in entirely different directions, we want them to grow into healthy, happy adults who have witnessed their parents enjoying prosperous lives at home and at work. In order to do that, we have had to discover how to use all our skills and flexibility to support them and each other. For instance, our freedom to be interchangeable is an illustration of what the women's movement

advocated over the last forty years — a sharing of time, energy and power between individuals, between the sexes, and encouraging men to step into responsibilities within the home as the women ventured out to exercise their talents.

Most couples have to create strategies for dealing with conflicting demands between the needs of family and the business. How do we act powerfully as partners at home and at work? What plans are in place to ensure one another's health and well being (e.g. physical exercise, creative and social activities, spiritual practice)? Do we have a vibrant network of support including family, friends and community?

When Children Are Welcome at Work: A Fortunate Situation

In some businesses, there is freedom to bring children to work when childcare arrangements break down, or even to expose children to what their parents do outside the home. This is a fortunate situation for parents and for children, as illustrated in the next two stories.

A few years after **Stacy Madison and Mark Andrus** [p. 36] divorced, Stacy started a family of her own and now has 7-year-old twin girls. When asked how having children influenced the business, they described their inclusive approach.

Stacy: The business was like a family. I think as a woman partner in business I had an advantage as compared to many other women in business. I had a partner in Mark who didn't mind when I periodically didn't have childcare and needed to bring the babies into the workplace. When our children were only 15 months, they basically ate chips!

Mark: I think it exposed them to a lot of people because they were brought in and were bouncing on my knees and socialized with other employees.

Stacy: Yes, they were good about going to other people instead of just chasing Mommy around. I was a single parent so it was really good to have everyone's support.

Barry Friedman and Valerie Gates [p. 68] also had a good experience including their children in their workspace.

Valerie: Our children have grown up with us working from home. When they were young, they would draw us little pictures, and once in a while Olivia would come over and put a picture on my desk while I was working that said, "You're working too much, Mom." They were very good about entertaining themselves from 3:00 to 5:00 in the afternoon when they got home from school, and now they do their homework in that time period. They have always been very good about being quiet if they were around when the phone rang. They know we all stop working at 5:00, so there's a clear boundary. They knew that after that time they could count on our full attention. We never hired babysitters or nannies because we never had to. They have always been able to roll with us. But I think it's been a benefit that we are around, especially if something happened.

Barry: Our 15-year-old son understands websites in terms of what they do and how we design them. He'll look over my shoulder every once in a while and say, "That's cool," or he'll sit on our extra computer and do his own illustrations, or try his hand at logo designs. When he was ten, there was a client who needed a child's drawing for a project teaching young children about alcohol abuse. So we asked him to draw a house. He did a great job!

Valerie: They get involved as much as they can, but they know that this is an office. Now our daughter practices being our "pretend" secretary. She even has a desk, laptop and phone.

Sometimes the Children Wait for Supper

Certain business structures and cultures enable children to come and go with ease. **Ron and Leslie Arslanian** [p. 65], on the other hand, talk about the difficulty of combining a successful mom-and-pop store with parenting. Their story highlights the issue of being torn between the worlds of business and family.

Ron: There are plenty of fathers that don't get to basketball games or soccer games, but then the mother's usually there. Having both of us at the same place really made it difficult for our kids. If either of us had been home to make dinner when Jamie came home, it would have been an entirely different story. The fact that we both weren't there made it harder for her.

Leslie: And there's that question — why wouldn't one of us leave? It's very interesting that it's not something I considered. Why didn't I just leave at 3:00 every day all those years so I could be home making dinner? We both felt this absolute need to be with one another at the store. We never really leave each other. We come and go together.

Ships Passing in the Day

For **Mark and Kate Friedman** [p. 67], too, it was difficult to balance business, children and their relationship. Their commitment to support one another and a sense of humor got them through some challenging times.

Mark: The weekends are killers. I see patients on Saturday mornings for four hours and then I know that I'm basically going to be doing childcare for the rest of the weekend. As soon as I come home on a Saturday afternoon, we high-five each other and Kate goes out the door.

Kate: I try to work it out that we have lunch together as a family. Especially at the time of year when wedding season approaches and I need to get deposits from clients. I try to tell people they can come in after 2:00 on Saturday. That way it gives Mark time to work until noon, come home and have lunch. I fill him in on the kids whereabouts, get to the office, unlock the door and turn on the lights to be ready at 2:00 pm to see clients. But literally it's a high-five or like ships passing in the night — except it's daytime!

Their story is an example of a relationship that suffered under the demands of raising a family while building two businesses that also involved a fair amount of charity and community work. In retrospect, Kate acknowledged that she was naïve, and has learned some painful lessons about what a relationship needs in order to thrive under conditions like these.

Freedom for Two Mothers

Knowing what they want and confidently pursuing their desires allows couples the freedom to fully enjoy life. The next couple emphasizes their intentional choices about choosing how much time they spend together so that they can be attentive parents and accomplished business owners.

MARY GILLACH AND KATHY HALLEY

Mary Gillach (51) and Kathy Halley (40) answered the call of their deepest desire, which was to create a relationship, a business and a family within a ten-year period. Partners since 1995, Mary and Kathy had a commitment ceremony in 1998, and in 2004, when it became possible for same-sex couples to marry in Massachusetts, they were married. They had their first child in 2001 and their second in 2003. While pregnant with their first child they launched their real estate business, FastGait.

Mary: We met as management consultants for a large firm. I had a series of credentials — a Masters in Physiology, an MBA from the Wharton School of Business — followed by ten years of consulting and executive roles. Waking up a month before my 30th birthday, I said, "I forgot to have babies, and this 110 hour week stinks!" I quit my job in 2000 and decided to get pregnant. Now I've been a realtor for four years and Kathy joined me for the last two years while also continuing as a consultant.

Kathy: I consulted for more than eight years and while it suited me in many ways, I hated it too. The work environment was terrible.

Mary: We always wanted to work together in our own business. We never knew what it was going to be. Part of our vision was having children and not wanting to be away from home five days a week.

Kathy: I missed Jordan's first year when I was in New Jersey on consulting engagements. I'd come home and cry about hating my job. Jordan would be six inches bigger and she would have so many new words. She would be clinging to Mary, and not to me. Now it's the other way around with Jacob. Mary breastfed her biological child Jordan for two years; Jacob is my biological child by the same father, the same donor, so they are related.

Mary: Our goal was to spend time with our family, have a good life and do something we believe in that helps people. We lucked into real estate. I was going to do it for four months until the baby came. The real estate agency that hired me when I was 5 months pregnant said it was against their better judgment because they anticipated my leaving after the baby was born. I just wanted to learn something new about investment property in the interim. We knew Kathy could take over financially with consulting while I tried something new.

Kathy: As it turned out, time passed, I gave birth to Jacob and was the at-home parent with the two children as well as being supportive for Mary, who has been a real estate junkie forever. Mary has visions of retiring in her fifties and we are trying to make that happen; we're making money faster now than before, when we had been in the corporate world.

When asked how being a lesbian couple had affected their business, Mary responded.

Mary: Our situation is unique to our industry, a product of where we are in this historical time and also where we live. If you interviewed a gay couple in real estate in Colorado, it would be very different. Everyone we work with knows that we are business partners and partner partners. They all get our Christmas cards. Since we are not hidden, we have eliminated one kind of stress in our business and personal lives.

Kathy: We're integrated into the society as normal functioning members. People accept us. They feel safe talking to us, largely because we have good relationships with people. But some people have also embraced us because we are gay. Often people don't know how we got pregnant or that the children have the same father. We talk about social things with people — topics outside of real estate deals!

Nobody knows me in this business; my identity is non-existent. Who cares? What do I care if anybody knows how much of the equation is my contribution?

I do not work for Mary. I work *with* Mary. I am a number two and I will be the first to say it. Being gay also has been a big part of that. Why do I care what the rest of the world thinks when most of the people are going to tell me I'm wrong or they are praying for my soul? I have become more confident, self-assured and loving of myself as I have lost my former identity.

Mary: It's really hard sometimes. As much as I love and value the skills that Kathy brings to our teamwork, I also feel it can get a bit crazy. At times I think I'd prefer that we were doing separate businesses. This combination really tests a relationship. You have to be committed to doing the business together and be solid in your relationship before you try.

Kathy: When you have a difference of opinion in your personal life, then you have to turn around and still function in the business with that person.

Mary: You also have to be strong in what you are doing while having a relatively equal voice in the business.

Flexibility and Strong Family Values

With a strong family value of being present for their three growing children, **Ron and Alina Chand** [p. 44] developed a plan for Alina to learn Ron's business and then enter into it in such a way that they could more fully share both business and parenting. They extended this value to their employee policies. By allowing employees to work flexible hours in order to handle family matters, they created a culture that aligned their business practices with their family values.

Alina: Other than the fact that it was practical for me to go into business with Ron from a business perspective, from a life perspective it's played an important role in giving me the freedom to make my own work hours. I could send the children off to school and be home when they came home. I could bring work home and do it in the evening, so I could leave to see their plays, which made our life very, very easy in that way. It also helped both of us see how tough it is for working parents with little kids. We always tell our employees that we know they need their jobs to support their families, but their families always come first.

I'm sure it was a little difficult for our children at times, because when the business was growing most of our vacations were business vacations. If Ron had to take a trip to California, that's what we would do — stay an extra few days, go to Disneyland — and that would be our vacation. The kids would sometimes have to sit through dinners with customers. It was good. They were wonderful and I think they learned a lot from that experience.

"Global Citizenship" Holds Family and Business Together

The context of the bigger picture, which includes teaching children the values of being global citizens, ties this couple's home and business together.

DOROTHY AND WAYNE STINGLEY

Dorothy (58) and Wayne (68) Stingley have been a couple since 1983 and married since 1990. They met at Werner Erhard Seminars Training, now known as Landmark Education. "We were doing 'get better, get smarter' programs to survive and to be successful," Wayne reports. When they met, he owned two McDonald's restaurants. Initially he didn't think it would work to have Dorothy in his business. They now own and operate 11 McDonald's restaurants in Arizona, all within fifteen miles of each other.

Dorothy: Our work gives us a powerful context within which to be connected to each other. Some couples are mainly connected through a family and raising their children, while for others creating this main connection could be as business partners. We are each related in some or all of these ways, but the bigger context is our trying to make a difference and being good global citizens.

Wayne: If you have a really big game to play, raising your kids and having your family and business work need to be held in the context of the bigger picture. You need to handle those things or you'll never achieve the bigger picture.

Part Three: Extended Family
Just as our children are influenced by us, so we were affected by the experiences of our parents and grandparents. Immediate and extended family shape our values, which provides the foundation for success in business and family life.

Social Values Shape their Business
This couple shares a long, fascinating and satisfying story about the impact of family values and circumstances.

PETRA KRAULEDAT AND PETER HANSEN

Petra Krauledat (56) and Peter Hansen (69) are the joint owners of PointCare Technologies, Inc. In the late 1980s they became a couple and simultaneously went into business together. Neither Petra nor Peter came from entrepreneurial families. However, their reaction to certain family circumstances, and their orientation towards family social values, were what enabled them to be successful risk takers in business.

Peter: My parents and my childhood were important. My mother was a Boston native of Canadian and English descent, and my father was a Danish immigrant. They got married fairly late in life, so I was the only child. My father actually had little or no education, maybe second grade, and my mother finished high school. We lived with my Canadian grandmother, who had no schooling at all, so this was a household where education wasn't emphasized. The neighborhood was blue collar. Almost everyone worked at the former Bethlehem Steel Shipyard in Quincy.

I was a community project. There were several neighborhood women who were teachers, and they recognized that there wasn't that much going on in my house with regard to formal education. People would just more or less grab me off the street for impromptu afternoon sessions to teach me music, math, English and other things

It does take a community to raise a child. I look back on it and it really worked for me. My parents' strong political beliefs also influenced me. They were not prominent people. My father was a merchant sailor. Almost everybody in the merchant marines was Communist, especially if they worked below decks. He brought those beliefs home with him and they sat well with my mother and with my grandmother. I think the most important thing that came from that exposure was a strong sense of social responsibility.

Petra: Peter's Dad told me that he actually wanted to go into the garbage business with Peter, and he still to this day doesn't understand how Peter made it through Harvard.

Peter: They were good parents. They really cared. I have absolutely no complaints about my childhood. It was formative, especially in terms of my social and political view of the world.

Petra: I have a similar background, even though I was brought up in a more middle class environment. I was born in Germany right after the war. When I was 1½ years old my father died of war-related health problems. He was a prisoner of war into the 50s, and he came back a very sick man.

The war had disrupted Germany so significantly that there just wasn't much money to go around. But my grandfather was fiercely keen on opportunity. He pushed me into school and told my mother that I had to go to the highest level of education.

Petra: My grandfather was also a great presence in our family. He really dominated the family. My mother had a basic high school education and was not an intellectual, though she was a kind, caring and very protective woman. My grandfather was a true intellectual, very philosophically inclined. He had me read Kant and actually got me to understand what he was talking about.

Peter: That's a major achievement in itself. I wish I'd had him around when I was in college.

Petra: He did shape my life in so far as I have a socialistic bent. I do believe in helping people, but I think you have to give them the tools to fend for themselves.

I left Germany at age 31 because I was looking for opportunity. There you stay in the company you work for and have this smooth, very flat career. You get your 5% raise every year, you have health insurance; everything is really taken care of. I had landed a really good job at Hoechst, but I said to myself after five years, "I don't want to do this until I'm sixty-five — that's over thirty years!" I wanted to run screaming. I couldn't see doing that.

Being brought up and educated in Germany, I didn't even know what starting your own business meant. I was just looking to do something different. My company had foreign assignments, so I thought I would go somewhere just for a couple of years and then see. I came here by myself with no particular plan but with an open mind. After about six months I decided this was the place where I would find the opportunity I wasn't getting in my own country. It's worked for me so far!

The Love of Parents

The love of their parents and the courage of their grandparents enabled these next two couples to go into business and to experience great success. **David Nicholas'** parents believed in and supported their son and his marriage partner, **David Miranowicz**, [p. 48].

David Miranowicz: His parents are amazing!

David Nicholas: I have been fortunate and blessed. Growing up, I had many friends who were thrown out of their homes and disowned. In the seventies, gay people were in the worst of situations. They were forced to live on the streets and do any job. Many attempted suicide.

There was a transition in the eighties but then, with AIDS, life got difficult again. Now with gay marriage, there is some hope. It seems like every other decade we take a deep dive; maybe you have to go backwards to go forward. But my parents have always been supportive of me. After raising six kids, my mom retired from working at the ripe age of seventy-five. I do take care of my parents. We go to the movies together. We are both friends with our parents, which is very unique. We are so fortunate to have such great relationships with them.

We took my mother out for my birthday to see the Boston Gay Men's Chorus and the theme was love and marriage. I want her to be a part of the best times in my life because she had to witness all the years of me being teased, pushed, shoved and worse. I feel my mother can now rest in peace when her time comes. She knows that I'm comfortable and in love and being taken care of in a state that does recognize gay marriages.

David Miranowicz: What a miracle, to be where we are now!

The Courage of Grandparents

Where do couples get the courage to take risks? For many, it's an inspiration from the families they grew up in. **Richard Rosen and Marguerite Piret** [p. 22] offer us both inspiring and epic stories of their courageous and entrepreneurial grandmother and grandfather who came from different parts of the world. Richard's grandmother brought her family out of a dangerous wartime situation and took them to America to experience growing up in another culture entirely.

Richard: My father was a Lithuanian immigrant of Jewish origin who came from a little town next to Vilnius, one of the great Jewish cultural centers in the world. He had a very interesting trip to the United States. He left in 1914 with five brothers and sisters and his mother. They were going to stay in Lithuania and unfortunately for them World War I broke out. The Germans attacked Lithuania. My grandmother felt it wasn't safe, so she moved the family from their farm into the town of Ryazan, about 200 kilometers southeast of Moscow, where her sister lived. She had previously left one daughter with her sister, who had sons but didn't have a daughter. This, by the way, was a common thing in that era, to redistribute the children.

Marguerite: Or child, if one member of the family didn't have any children. This also happened in my family in Germany — one daughter was sent from Cologne to live with a childless sister in Wisconsin.

Richard: They stayed there for three years, and my father attended the Russian Orthodox school, the best school in Ryazan, as the only Jewish person and the only person who every morning stood there and did not bow down to Christ. This tells you what kind of person my father was. When he was twelve they left Ryazan because the Russian Revolution further distressed my grandmother, and she had to leave. They couldn't go west since World War I was going on, so they decided to cross Siberia.

In order to survive this journey, my grandmother knew that she needed to have a business to generate income along the way. She had money, so she purchased baking wagons and baking equipment, and baked breads, cakes, pastries, all the way across Siberia, from Omsk to Tomsk to Irkutsk and then down through Mongolia to Manchuria to Harbin, then to Port Arthur, a Russian enclave, and then to Kobe, Japan.

Meanwhile they lost track of my grandfather, so they stayed in Japan for about two years. He had left for the United States and, with all the turmoil, they lost communication. Finally the Japanese government figured out that he was in Seattle. They found my grandfather and notified him, then paid for them all to go to Seattle, Washington on the Chicago Maru, a vessel with a name now well-loved by my family.

Marguerite: The Japanese government gave them the financial credit to make this voyage.

Richard: When he came to the United States, my father started out as a butter and egg man and also bought wool from farmers. One thing led to another, and he became a salesman for a manufactured product, which taught him a lot about dealing commercially. My immediate family, and all my cousins and relatives, were one way or the other in manufacturing or a similar business; they were a very commercial family. Everybody was in business for themselves.

Marguerite: A lot of them were in the shoe business, since New England had a large shoe industry.

Richard: At the end, they owned multiple shoe factories with 1,100 people, 1,500 people, 700 people in Maine, New Hampshire and Massachusetts.

Marguerite: At Richard's Dad's ninetieth birthday there were old movies that I'd never seen. They showed his family on vacation; the whole family, including eighty-eight first cousins, would take over a New England hotel. But what I find interesting is that, not unlike the Boston Brahmins, they financed each other. They were all each other's partners, and they all supported each other; there was no other money for them. In the early years, they couldn't go to the Boston banks, where I worked. Eventually they did, but not for venture capital, not for starting a new factory.

Richard: They got their financing from the United Shoe Machinery

Company. My grandmother was fascinating. She was a master baker. She made the best stuff I ever ate in my life. I remember as a kid she never worked from a recipe... not once.

Marguerite: My mother is from Little Falls, Minnesota, and she grew up with Charles Lindbergh in a town of eight or nine thousand people. Her mother was Polish, and her father was German, I think almost 100%. He died on her nineteenth birthday. Her father's father had been mayor of the town, and the family had a bank, a little commercial bank in Little Falls. My mother got a master's degree in microbiology, and went to work at the University of Minnesota Hospital. As an anatomical pathologist, she worked in the hospital preparing slides.

My father was actually born in Winnipeg, but his parents had emigrated from Sprimont, a town near Liege in Belgium. He grew up in St. Paul, Minnesota, where I was born. He was a professor of chemical engineering at the University of Minnesota. He had a whole series of patents and products, many of which are still used today, and most of which were commercialized through Minnesota Mining, 3M, where he had worked before he decided to become an academic. I would say that I was raised in an environment of real tolerance, an integral part of the value system for my mother's family, and for my father's. I think that may also be partly a result of the Minnesota culture.

Interviewer: How did your history affect how you conduct business?

Marguerite: Our history affected our business in terms of giving us a strong value system. Integrity was always key. For both my dad and my mother, achievement was also important. The scientific method, basing conclusions on data as opposed to other things, was central. And cultural tolerance: when I was ten, we moved to France and I grew up as a French person. You have to be very open to become immersed and part of another culture, because it's transitional — it's very different from the U.S.

This experience has given me the capacity to look at things from vastly different points of view and value systems. It has enabled me to view different methods of looking at situations and evaluating them. This is certainly important in investment banking, where one of the key skills is the ability to reconcile vastly different points of view and successfully address the interests of different parties.

Aging Parents Complete the Circle of Life

When we are blessed with community, we have the kind of support we need as we face the challenges of attending to aging or dying parents, to sick or disabled children, or to chronic illness — all while running a business and keeping our couple relationship and family intact.

MARION DAVIS AND GINGER BURR

Marion Davis (56) and Ginger Burr (54) met when Ginger was invited to be a guest on a radio show that Marion hosted. Marion and Ginger have been together for 9 years and married for three. Marion is Executive Director of an agency called Self-Esteem Boston. This non-profit organization offers self-esteem educational groups to men and women coming out of recovery programs, as well as professional development training to service agencies. Ginger has a business called Total Image Consultants, and works on self-esteem from a different angle, helping people to be authentic and express themselves in a way that represents who they truly are.

Marion and Ginger volunteered the idea that Marion's mother would hold a place in the center of their lives. Several nights a week are spent in the nursing home with her where they thoroughly enjoy the community they all created.

Ginger: We tend to be fairly quiet people when we have downtime. We both spend a lot of time with people during the day, and then again in the evening at the nursing home.

Marion: The nursing home is a source of entertainment for me. I love going there and entertaining people. We have devised something we call Whoopee Cushion Therapy. I started bringing a Whoopee Cushion and a bag of disguises and funny things to try on, including fake teeth and mustaches. There is a group of "with it" women that gather around us.

Ginger: Ninety-three years old and totally there.

Marion: I've become friends with another woman whose mom also lives at the home. We bring this group of women together outside the confines of the lobby in an area that is protected, and they take turns sitting on the Whoopee Cushion.

Ginger: One woman has no legs, another has Parkinson's; yet they are able to pull themselves up on their arms and sit on the cushion.

Marion: They think it's a riot.

Ginger: They listen for who can make the most realistic sound. They love it and we have fun.

Marion: Bathroom adolescent humor brings laughter which heals. It's very satisfying to know that we can help people laugh about stuff they have to deal with every day.

Helping Parents Die at Home

Death as well as birth is a family event in many cultures. If we have close relationships with our parents, many of us would choose to be with them as they are aging and eventually dying. With proper available care it can be a blessing to be able to say our final goodbyes in the comfort of the home. The Daytners had the opportunity to do just that. **Allen and Theresa Daytner** [p. 46] brought both of her parents into their home and cared for them as they were aging and dying.

Theresa: We juggled seven children and have managed the care of ailing parents — all during the course of our business startup years. The first three years of our business were really flat; we ran one to two projects at a time for personal reasons. My father and mother lived with us. My father was dying of cancer and we had babies all over the place. My mother has MS. My father was taking care of my sick mother and we were taking care of my parents. I was the primary caregiver and manager of all these people. My father died in October of 2004, and for eight months my head was not in the game of the business.

I went away to Idaho for a month in the summer of 2005 with my four youngest children, changed the scenery, cleared my head and came back with a fire in my belly and a huge commitment to the business. We had an opportunity to bring a full-time, live-in nanny, the right person at the right time, into the apartment that my parents had vacated when my mother had gone into a nursing home. We were finally able to focus on the business in 2006. It grew by 800% over the prior year. With that growth, we had new employees. Now we have twelve employees including ourselves. We moved the business outside of our home and created a whole new ballgame.

Allen: We have been able to position ourselves so we can do it all.

Our Perspective on Family

We all begin by being part of a family. Family experiences and the stories we carry about them shape us all through our lives. Family relationships can be the most satisfying and also the most frustrating. One way or another they are often at the center of our lives.

This conversation focused on the intersection between family and business, and included stories about the inspiration and motivation of family, the positive influences of extended family, and the benefits for children. Also highlighted: the challenges of integrating work and family, and the sources of support that need to be in place for it all to work through each stage of life.

Just as the Golnicks began this chapter by stating, *"At the heart of our work is love of our family and the relationships within our family,"* we conclude with that same thought. From a love of family and a love that matures in relationships, the couples we interviewed have created productive and exciting businesses and have also made magnificent contributions to the world. The work of family and business influences and enriches the experience of community service, which we address in depth in Chapter Seven. Each area of life has benefited from the impact of the other.

Chapter Takeaways

1. Describe the family experiences or stories that influenced you to be in a business with your partner.

2. Examine what you are teaching your children about family and business and what they are teaching you.

3. Reflect on lessons you have learned from the opportunities and challenges of juggling family and business that could guide another couple in beginning a business today.

4. Share with another couple the wisdom you have received from your extended family and aging relatives.

"*Listening is a magnetic and strange thing, a creative force.
The friends who listen to us are the ones we move toward.
When we are listened to, it creates us, makes us unfold and expand.*"

—SHEL SILVERSTEIN (1930–1999)
AMERICAN ARTIST, MUSICIAN AND AUTHOR

CHAPTER FOUR

POSITIVE COMMUNICATION: FREE TO BE FULLY SELF-EXPRESSED

L ISTENING CAREFULLY AND SPEAKING THOUGHTFULLY to each other are the essential elements of good communication between any people. They are especially important for couples in business together who spend so much time with each other every day.

Cultivating communication is an art and a science, and the foundation of a healthy relationship. What we don't say and the ways we behave can sometimes communicate more than what we do say.

One of the most rewarding skills you can develop is authentic and complete communication. This includes communication of:

- Information
- Concerns and issues
- Conflicts and disagreements
- Feelings or emotional experiences
- Personal or professional needs
- Plans or solutions to problems
- Stories and humor
- Love, acknowledgement and appreciation

In this chapter we'll explore the idea of complete and authentic communication: how you can communicate effectively by learning how to listen actively and reflectively, and how to speak both directly and honestly.

The Essence of Communication

As we all know, respect, integrity and empathy are essential for a loving and trusting relationship. Respect is valuing people for who they are and treating them accordingly. Integrity is honoring your promises and communicating when you have to change them. Empathy is the ability to hear, see and feel the other person's reality as they experience it.

Communication Artists

This next couple has blended their design and business talents to create a remarkable relationship based on authentic communication, joy and empathy.

WYNN AND DOUGLAS WAGGONER

Wynn (65) and Douglas (61) Waggoner, from Boulder, Colorado, both artistic and entrepreneurial, are deeply grateful for their relationship. In 1996, they jointly founded The Naturally Fallen Timber Company, with a commitment to honoring the beauty and abundance of nature and expressing it through art. Douglas is the creator of Naturally Fallen Timber's furniture and wall accessories.

In 2005, Wynn expanded her innate artistic vision to establish a complementary business. Wynn Interiors and Intuitive Design uses her natural abilities with color application and textural design to enrich and beautify diverse environments. Married for 15 years and each in their second marriage, they exemplify the possibility of an extraordinary relationship — one that is intentionally created and differentiated from their past intimate relationships.

Wynn: From the very beginning, one of the key factors in our relationship has been our commitment to unconditional love and completely authentic communication with each other. There is nothing I can't say. That, for me, is amazingly empowering. With Douglas I have an opportunity to be myself in a way I never had before.

Douglas: That absolutely speaks to my way of being with her as well. I did not want things to be as they were in my previous relationship. Wynn creates an open space to step into... it's a natural occurrence and it's effortless. Maybe there is effort on her part because she's generating it, but for me it just occurs. We have formed a relationship that was nonexistent in any other relationship that we had.

Clearing the Way for Complete and Authentic Communication

Many of the couples we interviewed alluded to differences and conflicts, and referenced the significant amount of communication it can take to work through these issues in order to reach a satisfying result. Let's address some of the pitfalls most couples encounter along the way.

Much of the confusion and conflict is not in *what* you say (the content), but in *how* you say it. Your nonverbal signals/body posture, the tone of your voice, and the rhythm and cadence of your speech sometimes communicate more than your words. In addition, more often than not, people listen with "half an ear" or listen through the static of their reactions or judgments about the speaker or the message.

If you listen from your assumptions about one another rather than from an open mind and an open heart, your partner can sense that she or he is not being heard and may react either verbally or nonverbally. Anger, resentment or other feelings about not being understood often reappear later in an argument about another seemingly unrelated issue.

Without realizing it, couples often stop listening to each other. We start listening to our own stories and conclusions about each other, and this kind of disrespect leads to a loss of aliveness in our relationships. The voice of judgment and language of blame — "you always" and "you never" — can also become a regular part of our internal chatter about each other and the strategy we routinely employ in order to win an argument.

How do you begin to alter these habits so that you can communicate authentically and feel satisfied with the quality of your exchanges with your spouse or with other people?

Start by listening to yourself. Listening to yourself demands a willingness to breathe deeply, quiet your judgmental mind, acknowledge the "you always" and "you never's that were bubbling below the surface, based on past experience. Let those go and listen differently without the need to prove you are right — whether or not you think you are. Only in altering the mindset and offering that kind of listening can you truly hear what the other person is saying, feel the other person's emotions, and then respond consciously and intentionally. Only then will both parties experience effective and joyful communication.

Models for Effective Listening

How do you listen to each other in personal or business conversations? In his book *Theory U*, Otto Scharmer[1], suggests that there are four ways we can listen:

1. Downloading information and habits of judgment which confirm our opinions and judgments;

2. Factually: noticing differences, listening with an open mind and disconfirming new data;

3. Empathetically: listening with an open heart, making an emotional connection and seeing through another's eyes;

4. Generatively: listening with an open will, from the space of future possibilities, connecting to the emerging future whole, being open to a shift in self-identity.

Charles Kiefer[2] of Innovation Associates, Inc., based in Sudbury, Massachusetts, suggests two ways of listening: one is to listen for confirmation of what you remember hearing before, and the other is to listen for communication that triggers fresh thought or insight — the kind of thought that comes suddenly and provokes an "Aha!" experience.

There are many other models for effective listening that translate into constructive ways of speaking and support satisfying communication. These two models offer pathways for deeper, more reflective listening, which in turn can free you from what Scharmer calls the three enemies of clear communication, namely the voices of judgment, cynicism and fear.[3]

The Context for Successful Communication

All couples create a context for communication. For some, it is one of cooperation and engagement; for others, it is an environment of conflict and resistance. Obviously, the environment that both partners create can either enhance or hinder the vibrancy of your relationship and the profitability of your business.

---

[1] Otto Scharmer, *Theory U: Leading from the Future As It Emerges* (Cambridge: Society for Organizational Learning, 2007).

[2] Charles Kiefer, from *Entrepreneurial Thought and Action*, a course co-sponsored by Innovation Associates and Babson College.

[3] Otto Scharmer, from *Presencing Institute: Capacity Building Online Global Classroom*. (September, 2009).

The Power of Partnership

The relationship between **Sandy and Lon Golnick** [p. 58] provides a powerful example of successful communication.

Sandy: It's a joy to live with Lon in our marriage. He brings partnership everywhere, even though he talks about being a lone ranger. He gets up in the morning and makes breakfast and looks ahead. I've never been so cared for by anyone. I feel so blessed to have the kind of partnership that enables us to look at the other's world. In our relationship, it's the best gift I could have been given. In our work, I treasure Lon's ability to look beyond what is either written or said. He is a rigorous listener. I often find myself wanting to communicate something and I just blurt it out. Lon, on the other hand, will give some thought to it and then have a magical impact on people.

We balance each other quite well. We love teaching together because we see things in alignment and complement and empower one another. When we are leading a course, people will say, "Lon's doing a lot of the talking, what about you?" The joke of it is that it doesn't occur to me as one or the other. As far as I'm concerned, it's WE talking. It may be coming out of his mouth or out of mine, and most of the time we don't know who is speaking!

Ambassadors for Plenty

MATTHEW AND TERCES ENGELHART

Terces (60) and Matthew (54) Engelhart are the owners of Café Gratitude, a group of unique raw food restaurants in the San Francisco Bay Area and in Los Angeles that are designed to provide healthy and delicious raw foods and educate people about them. They have written three well-received books and offer workshops and seminars. They created a beautiful board game, The Abounding River, which offers players a journey into self-worth, gratitude and abundance. The island of Maui in Hawaii is their second home where they have an organic farm and hold yoga retreats. In addition to copreneurs and co-authors, they are also parents and grandparents. Here is how they describe the context for their working partnership.

Terces: Our day-to-day events — my interactions, our relationship, our communication with employees, and the running of the business — are all guided and influenced by what we talk about in our book "The

Abounding River" (North Atlantic Books, 2007). What we think, speak and believe, how we act and our perspective are all ways of expressing ourselves. For us, this comes from the firm belief that this is a world of plenty. I don't get caught up in thinking. "There's not enough time, not enough money, not enough good employees, not enough time with my grandchild...."

Matthew: Or not enough love. Rather than focusing on my own preferences, needs or comforts, I ask myself the question, "If I were being the whole of life, or the whole life was being through me, how would love act in the face of this circumstance?"

Terces: I'm an ambassador for ushering in the idea that there really is plenty. When I catch myself personally getting caught in any expression of "not enough" or any expression of "there's something wrong," I deliberately focus my attention on being grateful, loving, accepting and generous. Practicing what we're sharing with the world is a moment-to-moment experience in all my interactions, whether it's family, business or recreation.

Larger Forces that Shape our Conversations

Besides our loyalties to the familiar patterns and dynamics of the families in which we grew up, the ways in which we communicate in business and intimate relationships are shaped by many other factors. These include our gender, class, racial and ethnic backgrounds, religious beliefs, health and able-bodiedness, and our gender preferences.

While an in-depth discussion of each of these factors is beyond the scope of this book, these are significant elements and we want to highlight some important ways they factor into the ways in which we communicate. Your background has a direct impact on the choices you make in your relationships and in your business. In some instances, race, gender or class plays a prominent role in building or expanding a thriving business. Success in business can also afford you the opportunity to be an advocate for others with less power, position or advantage.

The following stories speak to the issues of race, gender and class.

Significance of Race

Dorothy and Wayne Stingley [p. 76] are an interracial couple who, as they expand their successful McDonald's business, consistently advocate for a greater ratio of ethnic ownership and management throughout the franchise. Their goal is an equal proportion of black and white people, since that ratio more realistically and fairly represents the general population.

Wayne: One day a fellow school teacher brought me an application. He said that McDonald's was looking for minorities, but I wasn't interested. I was happy being a schoolteacher, working with 200 kids and making a difference in their lives. But then someone suggested I could use this opportunity to make a bigger difference in more people's lives by helping people make money and making money for myself, which would also mean I'd be in a better position to take care of my children.

I went for the opportunity, and became the 124th black McDonald's owner operator. I remember that number because that was 30 years ago, and today there are still only about 300 black McDonald's owner operators. Did we make any progress? Maybe. That small number did double, but still leaves much to be desired.

At that time the percentage of operators was far less than the percentage of black people in the population. We wanted 12% of McDonald's operators to be black or minority. We wanted that for blacks, Hispanics, Asians and everyone. It's sort of an unwritten rule to keep in the forefront at McDonald's: are you doing what you need to do to support your customer base? If these are your customers, and this is their ethnic breakdown, do the operators show up similarly to the ethnic breakdown of the customers? We are not afraid to take on or ask racial questions. We work in a way that dignifies people.

Significance of Gender

Gender is a significant issue for **Philip and Katy Leakey** [p. 27] as they help the Maasai women of Africa support themselves and their families.

Philip: In terms of how the business affected gender roles among the Maasai, initially there was a lot of concern from the men about empowering women financially because there was insufficient understanding about what could happen. As we progressed, and the women began to bring in regular income, the men began to appreciate what we were doing and encourage us to give women more work. It was clearly stabilizing their communities. Women were busy at home and at work. Everyone appreciated the stability. Women could now support the family in terms of food and school fees for the children while the men could maintain the investment in their livestock. All around it's been a big win-win for everybody.

Katy: It has also allowed the Maasai to start other businesses or small enterprises for both men and women. We have seen an increase in political and family stability and general growth overall.

Philip: Another angle is that now work opportunities are more available for the kids and they tend to remain in the community rather than getting an education and then leaving for the cities.

Significance of Class

Understanding what factors shape us, being aware of our differences and honoring the diversity of our life experiences can give us power in all our relationships. We learn to value, respect and work with people as they are. Differences that can be the source of conflict can just as easily become the basis of strength and connections by appreciating people for who they are and for the diversity they bring into our lives.

Mark Andrus and Stacy Madison [p. 36], the creators of Stacy's Pita Chips, communicated clearly that when they owned the business, their doors were open to any employee who needed to discuss an issue. They spoke about their commitment to creating a non-hierarchal, democratic organization where each person was heard, regardless of job description, education, social background or family history. Addressing class differences was a priority for them: they walked around the floors, ate lunch with their employees and held regular team meetings to maximize everyone's participation in the business and their willingness and ability to contribute to its success.

Stacy: It's not work if you love what you do. And that's true, not just for us but for every person that works here. For them it's not work either because they love what they do. It's really not a typical work atmosphere. I think some of the struggle in other companies might be that people don't like what they're doing and don't enjoy coming to work.

Mark: As we grow bigger and bigger — and, yes, we're taking over a 180,000 square foot facility — the vision is still going to include "no neckties allowed." It's still going to be an open-door policy in my office whether a person is upper management or cleans the toilets. We all work together and want everyone to feel comfortable sharing ideas, thoughts and feelings. Much of this vision stems from our social services backgrounds, which is satisfying to bring into this business.

Constant Connection and Conversation

As part of a couple in a business *and* intimate relationship you must communicate in order to help all the elements thrive. While TV, magazines and newspapers highlight the fragmentation of the American family, you are modeling new ways of being in relationship. During our research, we've observed couples' successfully communicating and making plans.

Sometimes discussions about renegotiating agreements, contracts, fulfilling commitments to business vendors or even deciding who is going to attend a school play or soccer game can continue from morning till evening. It may involve re-clarifying expectations about an upcoming weekend where you had to cancel the family barbeque so that both of you could meet with an important client who was coming into town.

As a couple in business together, you intend to make it all work, day in and day out, no matter what the circumstances might be. Even when there are conflicts or serious disagreements you are still committed to finding a way to connect. Resolving differences and communicating consistently will more often than not contribute to your enjoyment of your joint enterprise. The process of constant connection reinforces itself and continues to yield great benefits.

Constant Connection in Action

An abiding friendship and deep respect are at the heart of a couple's ability to keep communicating, even when the going gets rough. **Ron and Leslie Arslanian** [p. 65] have been best friends since they were teenagers.

Ron: Overall it's definitely a plus. There's no doubt about that. But again there are times when you can understand why most people don't work together because it's such a lot of time to spend with one another. I've talked to many people in small businesses who say, "I don't understand how you can do it." My response: "It's not easy." Obviously we've done it for 26 years, so the bottom line is it comes out...

Leslie: ...more positive than negative.

Ron: But it doesn't mean that the negatives along the way sometimes don't result in arguments. Well, the negative would be carrying it on at home. And instead of two business owners disagreeing about something, it becomes an argument between a husband and a wife.

Leslie: However, the nice part about it is that there is a continuity of our day life into our night life. We value our time at home together. We talk about what happened and what we went through during the course of the day. Most of the time it's as interesting a part of our evening as the day is.

And that's a good part. Sometimes it's just too easy for people to decide to get divorced because they have no bonds beyond the kids. When you have a business, that is another strong bond and an incentive to make it work. Do we have hard times? Do we get angry with each other? Absolutely. But divorce is not something we can ever conceive of, even if we're so angry at one another that I can't talk to him, or even if he's angry that I'm more in his face than he really wants me to be. Divorce is not in the cards because we have built a life around this entity and we are so proud of it. It was so difficult in the beginning because of the way we struggled running our mom-and-pop retail store in the early years. It was unbelievable. If we didn't get divorced then, we'll never get divorced. Beyond being husband, wife and business partners, we are absolutely best friends. We have been best friends since we were 15 and 16 years old, respectively.

People would have no idea that we can get as angry at one another as we do because we can literally be screaming at one another until we unlock General Optical. We walk in and it's "How are you?" to customers, I'm not kidding. It's the most unbelievable transformation you could ever see. If we were at home, we could keep that fight going for weeks.

Intimacy as a Communication Enhancer

Intimacy is fueled by friendship and in turn *enhances* friendship. Sexual intimacy is important and is just one way that a couple can be intimate. Each couple goes through a process of defining and creating their own intimacy practices.

Love Makes the World Go 'Round

ANTRA AND RICH BOROFSKY

Antra (63) and Rich (69) Borofsky, a Cambridge, Massachusetts co-professional couple, explain that they are more like artists and lovers than business people. They work together in their psychotherapy practice and lead retreats and workshops called *Being Together: The Art of Intimacy*. Trained respectively as a psychologist and a marriage and family therapist, they met in 1970 at a gathering of the Boston Humanistic Psychology Association and were married five years later.

Antra: We love the whole mix and messiness of life — its beauty, its pain, its possibilities and its limitations. Our practice is to include whatever is happening moment by moment, whether difficult or pleasing.

Rich: We have created a livelihood and a life and that grows out of this practice.

Antra: As couples therapists, we help people love each other. At the same time, we are engaged in the practice of also loving one another while we're working with them.

Rich: When we are working together, we use everything that's happening between us and between the couple partners to create a more compassionate and passionate connection. For example, we've learned how to use the energy of conflict as a vehicle for deepening love. Getting over our own fear of conflict has made us resilient and able to include and integrate both positive and negative experiences.

In their work, the Borofskys see intimacy as an essential practice, similar to the practice of meditation or singing or a high level sport. They believe that practice is how couples in long-term relationships can learn to expand their capacity for intimacy. In fact, many of the stories interwoven throughout this book also illustrate the practice of intimacy.

Using Personal Power in Communication

Playing with risk and edginess is another way to stay in communication and enjoy your relationship. This couple offers their unique view of play — openly acknowledging its power to create or destroy their relationship. Basically, everyone has the same power, but few people are as honest about it.

The Power to Make or Break a Relationship

JENNIFER CHRISTIAN AND DAVID SIKTBERG

Jennifer Christian (64) is an entrepreneurial physician, and David Siktberg (63) is a consultant and software developer. Married for 13 years (the first marriage for him, the third for her), they met when Jennifer needed to hire a systems person for a large healthcare company and asked David to help her write a job description to find someone like him. Today Webility Corporation is their own training and consulting company, and 60 Summits Project, Inc. is a nonprofit organization they founded and operate as well. Both are grounded in Jennifer's enduring interest in preventing unnecessary work disability. Originally aimed at a physician audience, they now focus on insurers and employers and continue to look for larger venues in which to communicate their message.

Jennifer: We realized years ago that we are both tremendously powerful people and that either one of us could destroy our relationship in half a day. It's incredible to realize that you have the power to destroy it or create it. This week we were having a disagreement and I actually said out loud "Do you want to wreck our relationship this afternoon or not?" We both agreed, "Oh, okay, NO!"

Productive Conflict: Having Difficult Conversations

We believe that couples who share their lives in such close proximity (sometimes 24/7, 365 days of the year) need to pay special attention to the relationship because the success of the business is directly connected to the power and clarity of their bond. Couples in business together recognize that they have to consistently keep their relationship issues clear in order to be effective business partners.

Couples who choose to work in separate jobs, businesses or professions have the luxury of finding refuge in work when the relationship is on shaky ground. When a couple is in business together, work is not a refuge from difficulties in the relationship. Creating and leading a business together can both enrich and complicate a marriage, an intimate relationship or a couple's partnership. The vicissitudes of business life can add to the mix of hopes and fears, expectations and obstacles that challenge any intimate relationship. The depth of love and respect can be tested by a downturn or conflict on the business side of things. When a business and a relationship are interconnected, these very same challenges can be magnified to the point where they threaten a couple's livelihood.

Directness, flexibility, negotiation, acknowledgement, the ability to apologize and a sense of humor are all important skills for making it through difficult conversations. Unhealthy anger and rage can fill a person with hatred and the desire to annihilate the other person. Sometimes when we fight, we are not seeking resolution but trying to dominate the other person. Sometimes we are more committed to being right than we are to clearly communicating our needs. Ultimately, we need to cool down before we can effectively address the issues that have stirred up the anger. We need to keep in mind that our primary goal is having our businesses and relationships thrive.

The Capacity to Appreciate Differences of Opinion

Ron and Alina Chand [p. 44] appreciate and even enjoy their differences of opinion. They also differ in their comfort with conflict. The capacity to hold divergent views and manage incomplete communication is rare and yet it is an essential element of establishing trust. This trust is the foundation of the willingness to "stay with it."

Ron: One unique thing about us and not easily understood is that neither one of us truly backs down. If we have a difference of opinion at some point we say, "Okay, we've had enough of this argument," and we are able to go on and be satisfied without one of us having to give in and agree with the other, because nobody is going to. She's never going to agree to something that she doesn't believe in. It's just the way it is.

Alina: It keeps our relationship interesting. After 31 years of marriage, we can go to a restaurant and we can talk nonstop all the way there and back.

Ron: I was never taught how to handle conflicts, so if there's a conflict at work, Alina is much better prepared. And if we discussed how we were going to handle it, we would never agree with each other's suggestions. We understand that about each other.

Practices for Handling Conflict Successfully

We must learn to handle the process of working out differences, which requires us to identify our needs and wants and to make them known by expressing them out loud. We all employ a variety of different strategies to protect ourselves, and vulnerability can easily surface. If we were raised in families and cultures that didn't support the direct expression of needs and wants, this can be difficult. Being more open with others cultivates feelings of trust, empathy and compassion.

In times of conflict, it is helpful to remember that you have a history together and have solved problems in the past. Also, it helps to remember that we are not fighting World War III. It takes practice to learn to use the powers of our minds, emotional intelligence and speech to negotiate for our personal gain while being an advocate for the good of the relationship and business. When we enter into positional bargaining, we want our position to prevail and we sacrifice our ability to be open and connected in the relationship. In other words, when we are being "right" we are committed to our own reality and have no interest in our partner's. Ultimately, the choice is ours. One approach to resolving conflict that works well for many couples is to give the relationship a vote in addition to their own individual votes. The relationship often casts the deciding vote.

Here are some practices that support and encourage directness, flexibility and the ability to negotiate, acknowledge and apologize even while you are in the midst of conflict. They may enable you to get back to remembering why you love each other and have a sense of humor about how maddening your partner can be.

While these are guidelines for handling conflict successfully, they can also be considered as appropriate behaviors to practice around any relationship issue.

Time and Place:

1. Take time to have a difficult conversation.

2. Create the physical space and necessary boundaries so both people feel safe having the difficult conversation.

3. Keep "fire fights" contained and separate from employees, customers, children or others who will not help resolve the conflict.

4. Choose your battles.

Speaking, Listening and Noticing:

1. Speak in "I" terms and behavioral terms to define feelings, experiences, needs and disagreements (e.g. "When you do X, I feel...").

2. Learn how to read your own and others' nonverbal cues for the feelings they are expressing. This includes facial expressions, tone of voice, body postures and movements that are congruent or incongruent with what both you and the other person are or are not saying with your words.

3. Remember that successful communication must be delivered in language that the other person can understand. Master the

art of finding and using the words that strike the right emotional tone.

4. Deliver requests and state agreements completely to avoid misunderstandings and resentments.

5. Make every effort to listen carefully to what is being said.

6. Stay eye-to-eye and attend to one issue at a time.

7. Avoid character assassination and phrases like "You always" and "You never."

8. Be respectful — remember that this person is an intelligent, competent human being, just as you are — even when you are really angry or frustrated with their attitudes, behavior or beliefs.

Break and Consultation:

1. If you need to take a break, agree upon a time to return and complete the argument or disagreement and clarify what you want.

2. Seek consultation when you are stuck — not just someone to support your position or take your side.

Larger Perspective:

1. Learn from your mistakes, be accountable and acknowledge when you have made a mistake.

2. Invent something new rather than rehashing the past — choose to move on rather than fight.

3. Remember this is a person you love (if not at the moment!), the one you chose to be your partner in business and life.

Letting Go and Moving On

There are many ways to handle conflict. We are free to choose how we want to act in each difficult situation that arises. Sometimes we jump in and sometimes we let it go. **Sandy and Lon Golnick** [p. 58] have a way of moving through and beyond conflict.

Lon: From time to time we find ourselves on the wrong page. We'll have a short blowup, and we don't constrain ourselves from doing that. If I find myself upset, I express it, and it's the same with Sandy.

Interestingly, we don't even work on it, but see it is an opportunity for expression rather than taking it too seriously. A lot of people think that if they have incidents where they get upset, something is wrong.

We've discovered that disagreements from time to time are a part of being related, and the harder you work on your problems, the more they are in front of you. We allow room for the distress. We are kind of like children — when they fall down and hurt themselves, a couple of minutes later it's forgotten. In our experience, success depends upon whether you deal with it from the past or from the future. From the past you hash it over; from the future you invent something new.

Appreciation and Acknowledgement

As human beings we yearn for love and respect. When a fundamental sense of trust and belonging is present, we experience connection and partnership. When these elements are missing, acknowledgement and appreciation can bring us back together. A context of caring provides a framework for resolving hurt feelings. It also cultivates a spirit of generosity within the relationship, which is a high yield investment in the future of the partnership.

Dr. John Gottman, a primary researcher in the field of relationship and couple communication, has shown that a couple needs to have six positive and validating responses to balance out a single negative one in order for a relationship to survive and thrive.[4]

This being said, we each need to acknowledge, appreciate, value and respect ourselves and address any difficult emotions or issues that undermine the partnership. Developing an "attitude of gratitude" is a good starting point. As you pause to recognize your own strengths, accomplishments or contributions, you can more easily acknowledge your partner's. Appreciating something particular about them or what they did that was helpful doesn't have to be a big deal or take a long time. It can often be simple and ordinary and take just a moment. What matters is that you do it in a way that is authentic for you and also rings true for the other person.

Acknowledging One Another

In our interviews, we asked each member of the couple about the strengths of their partner. For many, integrity is number one. It is a powerful gift to

---

[4]John Gottman, *Why Marriages Succeed or Fail: And How You Can Make Yours Last.* (New York: Simon & Schuster, 1994).

have a business partner that you can count on, someone who is in it with you 100%. Most couples will honestly admit that their business would never have gotten where it is without the contribution of the other. This is even true when they see each other's contribution as both the benefit and the blight of the business.

Our Perspective on Communication

A couple's success in business together depends upon their ability and willingness to communicate with respect, integrity and empathy in day-to-day situations and in complex negotiations where there may be conflict, challenge and risk. Genuine and effective communication can be a joy. It feels great to speak honestly and directly about what matters and to be heard completely. Use the important skills of listening carefully and speaking thoughtfully to foster authenticity, honesty and growth.

Chapter Takeaways

1. Assess your listening and speaking skills. Are there one or two practices that would allow you to be more powerful in either or both of these areas? Check this out with your partner.

2. Discuss with your partner how you complement each other to handle a variety of situations. Do you have a practice of acknowledging each other for your contributions?

3. What conversations about communication could expand or alter your relationship or the way you do business? Consider inviting other friends into these conversations about effective communication.

"They have achieved success who have worked well, laughed often, and loved much."

—ELBERT HUBBARD (1856–1915)
AMERICAN WRITER AND PRINTER

CHAPTER FIVE

WORK-LIFE INTEGRATION: MAKING TIME FOR SELF-CARE, PLAY AND MORE

L IFE IS FULL OF POSSIBILITIES and pleasures — family, friends, culture, nature, travel, physical exercise, spiritual explorations — internal and external adventures of all types. We all know it's important to take time for ourselves and our intimate relationships, yet the pressures of business can absorb all of our discretionary time.

This chapter offers insights into some of the ways that couples in business together enjoy themselves. From simple rest and recreation to special vacations to consistent daily practices, from cultivating intimacy to fostering family and supporting communities, from nurturing your own spiritual growth to expanding the possibilities for the next generation — the energy generated by these pursuits fuels a relationship and can reinvigorate a couple's business.

How do you integrate taking care of yourself, your relationship and the business? How does vacation time nurture you? How do you sustain the care of yourself and your relationship while fulfilling your long-term commitment to your business? How do you balance work and play, blend them or separate them in your life?

These are crucial questions for couples in business together. Answering such questions opens up opportunities for learning, growth and fun that strengthen us personally and support our business.

Play and Vacations

Time away from the ordinary day-to-day routines and responsibilities is a great way to take care of ourselves. Vacations are special times to disconnect from daily life, refresh ourselves in body, mind and spirit, and experience ourselves and our partners anew.

Creating Vacations

Vacations are a regular way that many couples enjoy and stretch their thinking. **Richard Rosen and Marguerite Piret** [p. 22] have enormous respect for each other's intellect and creativity. They view themselves as courageous travelers into the mind and throughout the globe

Marguerite: We're both brave. So we pique each other's courage to do different and unusual things. I've found Richard to be very supportive of me; if I want to do something, he finds a way to help me do it.

Richard: I can't imagine being married to anybody who would be more interesting and more of a challenge than Marguerite, except perhaps myself. We don't always see eye to eye, but we do see eye to eye on an awful lot of things which come very easily to us but give other couples enormous difficulty.

Marguerite: We like to travel. We both like to go to bizarre places that nobody else wants to go to. Letting everything in my real world go is, for me, a lot of fun. Shopping in the bazaars of Jordan, charging through Petra canyon with red walls into an ancient building called "The Treasury," exploring archeological sites...

Richard: People look at us and say, "Are you out of your minds?" We went to Bahrain, Jordan and Egypt just last year before Christmas, and we had a wonderful time.

Marguerite: No one was visiting because it was Jordan. People thought they would be attacked. It was fine and it was fun.

Richard: And people thought we were totally insane.

Marguerite: They don't know how wonderful these places are.

Richard: We've been everywhere. There's hardly a country that we haven't set foot in.

Like Marguerite and Richard, many couples enjoy exotic travel that takes them out of their everyday reality and gives them a greater appreciation for their life. Travel offers other ways of seeing the world and broadens you by giving you an opportunity to look at the cultural values you take for granted. Travel for most people is limited when the children are small, but as they grow older, some are able to combine longer vacations with working on the road.

Vacations are one of the many ways in which successful entrepreneurs **Wendy Capland and Chris Michaud** [p. 14] make space for play, separately and together.

Wendy: We have taken dance lessons off and on for many years. I love to do stuff with Chris. We have our own individual interests too, but I'd rather do something with him than do something alone because we just love being together. We ski together on the weekends. We vacation extremely well together. We just came back from ten days in Costa Rica. It was great. What else do we do to play? We love walking in the woods together. We love going out to dinner.

Chris: We also have people over. We like entertaining and being with good friends.

Playtime Each Month

David Nicholas and David Miranowicz [p. 48] are experts at creating short times away each month. They speak about taking time off from work responsibilities to enjoy each other, family and friends and make the time for other creative outlets.

David N.: Typically in the beauty industry there can be a lull in January, February and July. That's when we'll fit in time to go away or upgrade our business to a new level, redecorate the house or whatever we choose. In the 30 years I've been in business I think I've had seven work week vacations.

David M.: And I was the one who initiated them!

David N.: I never used to take time off. Two or three-day jaunts were about the extent of it. I've never had two weeks off in my life. I couldn't do it. I'd be too uncomfortable. We try to take two or three-day jaunts once a month. We succeed maybe half a dozen times throughout the year. But remember, not every work day is 16 hours. There will be days that are just 4 hours long where we juggle everything — work, family, play — it's all intermingled for us.

An element of play and fun has surfaced in each of the stories in this chapter. But it does not work in the same way for everyone.

Work as a Source of Renewal

Relaxation can be a state of mind as well as a physical and emotional experience. We see expanded possibilities for relaxation very clearly in the way individuals within a couple think about caring for themselves. Each person knows how to take care of themselves and get what they need. One person may simply work out, eat and sleep to relax. The other may find their work to be a source of renewal and creativity. Even when they are trapped in an airport, sleeping on the floor, they remember that their work is a privilege, and when they're home they may play, relax and have fun just being with their family and the people they love.

Caring for Ourselves with Daily Practices

Meals and Rituals

The cooking and sharing of food is one of the primary ways that people from almost every culture express love and caring. This is certainly true for this next couple, who add the ingredient of meditation to flavor their cooking.

ROSI AND BRIAN AMADOR

Rosi (51) and Brian (52) Amador are accomplished musicians who live in Cambridge, Massachusetts. They met and fell in love on a cultural exchange trip to Nicaragua, and returned to start a business and a relationship all at the same time. Together for 26 years and married for 23, they are parents of 15-year-old twin daughters, Sonia and Alisa. Their primary business is a band called Sol y Canto, whose music promotes and celebrates Latin culture. Now that the girls are in high school, they have made the decision to take a hiatus from touring and shift their focus towards their secondary business, Amador Bilingual Voiceovers. Rosi and Brian spoke about what they do to support themselves in their personal life.

Brian: Cooking is a huge source of support for me and for Rosi. I cook every day. It is a very meditative process for me.

Rosi: He is truly a gourmet chef. The girls and I are very aware of it. Every day we express our gratitude.

Brian: Another source of support for me is my family — just being able to spend time with Rosi and my girls. I feel very fortunate to have a loving, joyful and satisfying relationship with my children.

Rosi: We have always prioritized creating downtime. We work so hard when we work and we need downtime. I have always been very effective in planning vacations. Often they are intertwined with work, but not always, and those times are healing and nurturing for us as a family and as a couple. When we think about our future and money, we think we have to put it away, and it's always a great conflict. Do we go to Mexico or another place nearby? Do we give our daughters the cultural enrichment which we think is so important, or do we put money away? I tend to be the one that favors living in the present. If you work at home, the e-mail, the cell phone... everything is clawing at you. But because we are mostly self-employed, we've also been able to fashion vacations that have been incredibly helpful in sustaining us.

Lynne and Bill Twist [p. 23], global activists, were reminded about the importance of taking time to relax around meals when Lynne read Paul Dolan's book, *True to Our Roots: Fermenting a Business Revolution.*

Lynne: In Europe, the value system is about having leisure time and living a good life. But here in America the value is productivity. For example, the Dolan family tradition was to stop and have dinner with a glass of wine. The theory is that after you have a glass of wine, it's harder to work. It marks and completes the day — now it's time to generate free time to be with your husband, wife or your children. I never really thought this, but one of the things that keeps people from working too much in Europe is that they drink wine at dinner. They actually stop, sit down, have a glass of wine and a conversation. There is a ritual to it. It's beautiful — the food is important, every taste is essential, and they don't gulp down their food — they revere eating. This realization made a huge impact on me. I wanted to start doing that, having wine every night.

Bill: The wine is not always so necessary, but the dinner certainly is. Sitting down for dinner was an incredibly popular part of our American culture until the last twenty years, when we became a success-driven empire.

Lynne: In my family of origin it was really important, and I haven't maintained that practice in this family. My grandmother made a big thing about dinner. We lit candles; we could not take phone calls; we had three courses, silver, napkins. I have done a wimpy job of recreating that for my children and it suddenly comes back to me why we did it. I've forgotten how potent these simple rituals can be — setting a table, lighting a candle, pouring even half a glass of wine.

Bill: Having rituals really gets us back in touch with being related and gets us out of our task obsessions. It's actually very important. I didn't grow up with the silver, but I did grow up with all the other parts of the ritual. We did insist on our kids having dinner and our having dinner. That's a significant part of our family culture.

A Wide Range of Activities

Having a wide range of activities contributes to our sense of aliveness and challenges us to be constantly learning and growing. **Nick and Mitra Lore** [p. 25] spoke enthusiastically about the various activities they enjoy.

Mitra: To relax we see friends, and we are blessed with many children, as well as grandchildren, parents and siblings.

Nick: Mitra's the extrovert. She often talks on the phone, and she's constantly interacting with people.

Mitra: For socializing and getting together with people, I'm in charge. Nick trusts me and follows my lead. Or we take a nap or sit on the sofa with the Sunday paper, or watch movies on TV when we've had enough of people. We also love to travel. I dance salsa, I do yoga here and there and I've become a visual artist.

Nick: I play the guitar and listen to a lot of music. I love watching films and have a large oceangoing sailboat that I'm passionate about. And for me, where we live is magic: two and a half acres in such a quiet spot. I walk around and admire my landscaping and watch the fish in the pond I installed last year. I am curious about all sorts of things. I read several books at a time. I take photographs and create paintings from them. I like computer stuff and I inherited a love of shopping from my mother, so I am a frequent eBay visitor!

Reflect for a moment on your favorite time-out activities. How frequently have you made time for them in this last week, month or year? What is the right balance between work and play for you and your partner?

The Challenge of Balancing Work and Play

This couple, like many couples, experienced the challenge of discovering the right balance between work and play, especially in the early stages of growing a business.

REBECCA MARSTON AND ALEXANDER VOSS

Rebecca Marston (48) and Alexander Voss (38) met in 2003 when he was moving to Finland and looking for someone to manage his properties. He proposed eight days later, and they were engaged for several years, but never married. At the time of our interview, they had created Marston-Voss Realty, an up-and-coming Boston real estate company that handled property management, rentals, sales and development in Boston.

Alex: As life partners and business partners, we are challenged to find the balance by not overdoing it and making time for ourselves. Rebecca wants to go to a spa, I want to play golf or run or sail. We each need to have a private life that is not co-mingled and is separate from our work life. When we're home, it's time to take care of each other. It's so easy to overlap the two worlds and keep talking about work that we actually need to structure play time.

Rebecca: We now have a shared calendar and have included our workouts on the calendar. For now, vacations have come to a screeching halt.

Alex: Vacation is always outside of the United States. We like to go to Europe and Mexico. We both love to travel. Once the company is up and running we plan to go away several times a year, at Christmas and for each other's birthdays.

Now Rebecca runs the business herself under the name Marston Beacon Hill, and Alex runs his own company, Voss Development Group.

Rebecca: At the inception of a small business, sacrifice is one of the realities. I'm still working on trying to vacation, but the business is stable and successful.

When so much of the business involves travel, it can be more of a stressor than a source of recreation, as we learn from **Philip and Katy Leakey** [p. 27].

Katy: We do not relax enough or give ourselves enough time for ourselves.

Philip: We still need to take more downtime. We often work 15-18 hours a day and we get exhausted. Plus we travel a lot. The worst part of the business is being in airports and on airplanes. Sometimes we can get away to our small place on the coast.

Katy: This business started in our home and it grew so quickly that we didn't have the time to build it further away and contain it. There was no physical boundary between work and home, and we were determined to not let it happen again. Then we built a proper 5000 square foot workshop, and we live in a tented camp about two miles away. Since we moved our workplace far away from our home, it's much better!

Philip: We try to set aside a few hours at night, but sometimes we get so excited about the business that it just doesn't happen. Right now the most significant thing is to be of service and help to the people of Kenya. Land issues are close to our hearts. We believe that ownership of land is the key to stability, to peace in the world. I am involved with helping the Maasai improve their welfare and sort out their land issues.

Katy: I am devoted to my family in America and our family in Kenya. Coming from a close immediate family and an extended family of 75 people, we love to be together.

Separating Work and Play: Setting Clear Boundaries
How successful are you at putting boundaries around your work time or business conversations and making time for restorative activities? For some couples, ensuring clear separations between work and play is essential for the health of their relationship. The next two stories describe how two couples at different stages of their business and personal lives have managed the separation.

Peter Hansen and Petra Krauledat [p. 77] have been in a committed partnership for 22 years. They have intentionally put restrictions on their weekend time.

Peter: I think we've worked out a way of separating work and play. During the week, we start at seven in the morning and end at nine at night. We are not physically in the office or the lab all that time, but the topic of conversation is generally our work. We did figure out a long time ago how to turn the work part off on Friday night and turn it back on again on Monday morning. So weekends with no work have been a wonderful time as well. We really have managed to work this whole entrepreneurial thing with virtually no weekend work at all.

We've also enjoyed traveling together. We have a 99% rule that when we travel, we travel together. It's fun and we enjoy it. We always have a chance to go out and do something more interesting when we're together. It's been a good part of our relationship.

STEVEN AND MARJORIE SAYER

Steven and Marjorie Sayer have been married for 42 years and in business together as copreneurs since 1978. They have owned and operated four successful businesses in the course of their life together, from catering to consulting to cleaning. When we met them, they were preparing to sell Equipsystems, Inc., their 17-year-old innovative hospital cleaning business, in order to "retire." They were at a stage of their business where they were easily able to put boundaries around their work days. They stopped working during dinner time and devoted evenings and weekends to each other and their family. Their love of art, theatre and numerous creative outlets motivated them to stop work earlier than most people are able to do.

Steven: When we were first starting our businesses, our kids were younger, and Marjorie and I would sit at dinnertime and talk business. Our children found a way to break through and communicate to us succinctly and loudly, "We are important, your business is not (not now) and you are supposed to listen to us." Frankly, they trained us extremely well and they were 100% correct. Our focus shifted when the children were around, or when we had pillow talk. And we'd have Fridays, too.

Marjorie: Fridays we would shut down at 3 o'clock and go to the movies.

Steven: We'd try to get to the 4 o'clock show since there was nobody else there and all the new movies opened up on Fridays. Today none of the kids are around, and if we are not traveling on business and are at home, somewhere between 5 and 6 pm, we shut it down — that's the end of the regular business day.

Marjorie: One day I'll go back to painting.

Steven: We love to do our gardening.

Marjorie: We also read a lot. History inspires Steven. He loves *The New York Times*.

Steven: I don't always read, but when I kick into reading gear, I just consume. I'll stop to watch some particular TV shows... Grandchildren fully engage my attention at any time they want me. All they have to do is say "we want" and it's done!

Marjorie: I love travel and art. I'm very eclectic and like a whole variety of artists. Walking in the city inspires us.

Steven: We walked across the Brooklyn Bridge on New Year's Eve!

Now retired and living in Southern Vermont, their days are full, exciting and challenging in their "give back" mode. Steven is President of the nonprofit Board of Youth Services, mentors graduate school students at Babson College, and loves to ski whenever possible. Marjorie is on the board of the Vermont Humanities Council, mentors MBA graduate students at Marlboro College, and has returned to painting — one of her great passions — with shows in Vermont, New Hampshire and New York. They admit that they do not miss working!

Staying Grounded and Present

How often do you exercise or meditate? What good book have you read or great music have you heard lately? Being grounded in daily practices such as meditation, exercise, reading or listening to music is a wonderful support for self, partner and relationship, as this next couple demonstrates.

Rich and Antra Borofsky [p. 96] discuss the strengths each brings to their partnership.

Antra: The person from whom I learned the most about how to love myself was Rich's mother. She really knew how to take care of herself. I remember seeing her lying in a hammock on the deck of her seaside cottage with her earphones on, listening to a symphony and reading a book of poetry. She knew her favorite colors, her favorite music, her favorite foods, and she took great pleasure in them — I learned a lot from simply watching her.

Rich: The most important thing I've learned from Antra is how to be more generous. She has an extraordinary generosity of spirit. She is willing to give or do whatever is needed to make things work. She is an extremely positive person. She doesn't complain. I can't ever remember hearing her complain — which is amazing in and of itself.

Antra: One of the biggest benefits for me of Rich's Zen practice is his willingness to stay present and steadfast, no matter what is happening — whether it's pleasurable or painful. I am someone who has wanted to be comfortable. He has challenged me and taught me to stay openhearted, even when I'm in pain.

Another thing I treasure about Rich is his ability to see humor in any situation. This goes a long way in helping us gracefully manage the things that we have to deal with every day. He can be both serious and not, and that's a beautiful combination.

Passion and Intimacy

Passion and intimacy are core life experiences that have limitless expression in both work and play. For some couples it is more explicit and self expressed; for others it is more subdued and in the background. Many couples reported that their shared experiences create a bond that "juices" their intimacy. They find the expression of pleasure and joy in some of life's ordinary experiences, as we see in the next three stories.

Intimacy in Day to Day Life

Bill and Lynne Twist [p. 23] renew their relationship through a variety of activities, including taking regular walks in beautiful places, a course in meditation, and tango lessons.

Lynne: We took tango lessons with several other couples. It's not that we're great tango dancers, but we got into it. We would practice at night; we would turn on the music, and we had a tango video. The whole world of tango is like the world of our friends. It teaches you, and reminds you, that you are a woman and he is a man. And that needs to be, I think, constantly rekindled in our relationship, because we spend so much of our time working together.

Rich and Antra Borofsky [p. 96] also love to dance.

Rich: We love to dance. We often dance in the kitchen while we're cooking dinner.

Antra: And we do ice dancing. It's one of my favorite things to do together. We skate in dance position, looking into each other's eyes, listening to a favorite piece of music. I love looking into his eyes, and to be moving at the same time puts us on a physical edge. It's not easy — potentially it's dangerous — but it creates an extraordinary experience of concentration, surrender and joy.

Ginger Burr and Marion Davis [p. 83] reflect on what passion means to them and describe a playful ritual from their daily lives.

Ginger: Marion is passionate about everything she does, or she doesn't do it. Or she does it unwillingly. She has a sense of needing to be who she is, which can be edgy because she is not like everyone else.

Marion: You mean, in what seems traditional as a woman, or just in my thinking?

Ginger: All of it, everything. The way you think, the way you present yourself, the way you ask people questions that some people would be afraid to ask because they think it would be inappropriate. You're able to ask them in such a way that the other person feels not only compelled to answer, but also wants to answer. And you're the same in business. You bring passion to it, and you're incredibly intuitive; you have a gift for knowing when something feels right and when it doesn't.

Marion: One of the things we do that really keeps us having fun involves our physical chemistry. We have a little thing that we do every morning called "body part of the day." We tell each other the body part that we love about each other and why, and then an inner quality that we love. If we're not together, we leave a message on each other's voicemail, or I'll send Ginger a fax with funny drawings on it. This is a delightful way for us to begin each day.

Passionate People & No Boundaries

Ron and Alina Chand [p. 44] are passionate about business and each other. Seeing their business and personal lives as one has deepened their relationship.

Ron: I think business has brought us closer. As far as our intimate relationship is concerned, business has never really affected us. Alina and I are very passionate and private people. We've always been very passionate towards each other. Business could be doing well or it could be doing badly — it has no effect on us. When we are together we are together. It has nothing to do with anything other than us. We have not taken the business so seriously.

There is no boundary in our case. Our business and our lives are one and the same. So we have never looked at business as something good or bad that needs to be dealt with. It's just part of life: we go to the grocery store, we go to work. We take care of issues and problems as they happen. It has kept us very busy and active. Some people would say, "It's intruding on my tennis time. That's my leisure time so therefore I'm going to separate the business." Business is my tennis. I enjoy it. So it's not stressful, it's just busy. And Alina has recognized that I thrive on challenges and issues that are involved in the business world the way other people thrive on leisure time.

The Importance of Friends, Faith and Family

Re-Energize and Re-Create

The need to reenergize ourselves often gets us to step away, take a deep breath and re-create ourselves as we engage in activities we love or experiment with something new. Play as recreation usually includes any number of relaxing and invigorating activities that can happen either during the work week or on vacation.

Play as a time for the re-creation of body, mind and spirit is well-articulated by **Marguerite Piret** [p. 22].

Marguerite: The activities that allow me a sense of re-creation are my family, my nonprofit world and the world of the mind. I love to read literature. I read at night and also try to take a day off each week to read. I might go to our second home, lie down in bed and read a whole book. I love to read and think… and I like to argue about things. I think about current issues and have discussions about them, and I try to puzzle out how to solve problems as they arise.

I love to entertain friends. I love talking to people at a party, kayaking on a lake or going skiing, or going to the theatre where someone else is performing and I am not! Most of my life I have to perform, so it's a release from all that. I just get to observe, enjoy, think about it and relax.

The Role of Faith

The importance of faith and the sense of God within is as great a support for **Ron Chand** [p. 44] as human relationships are for his wife **Alina**.

Ron: On technical matters obviously we reach out to the technical people, but on business and personal matters my support has always been my faith. I have not known any other way to cope. I don't feel that I need to talk to a psychologist or a psychiatrist for any kind of stress that I may encounter…I can handle it through my faith. I have tremendously strong faith.

Alina: I don't have that kind of religious conviction and, as a matter of fact, sometimes I think maybe it's one of my weaknesses. I wish I had more of a religious fervor or pull. I believe in a God but I just don't find that kind of comfort in religion or God. I find it more on the human level.

Ron: Because I'm a scientist, because I'm an engineer, I have redefined God for myself. Some people will say you have to scientifically prove it, but I would argue that that's not necessarily the case because science cannot define joy, or laughter, or tell you what sadness is. There are no definitions in science for the human emotions, in which I think God plays a very important role. I don't see God as something outside sitting there in some form. I see God as within us. So I've redefined it all for myself and that's where I reach out when I need support.

Great Friendships and Family Relationships

There are huge benefits from nurturing our friendships and family relationships. These are people who come to know us intimately over time — our strengths and our vulnerabilities — and still love us. Their care and support can be an asset beyond measure. A number of couples have already commented on their importance to their well-being.

Allen and Theresa Daytner [p. 46] of Maryland have many friends who care about them and about their marriage and family. Coming from very different cultural backgrounds — hers is Latin American and his Russian — they have similar working class roots. They are committed to translating hard work into smart thinking and creating residual income from their company so they can travel.

Theresa: I don't have any trouble asking for assistance. My adopted aunt lives with us. She is an incredible woman, and our relationship means a lot to me and our family. I also brought one of our first employees into our personal life; a woman I trust, respect and want to also help grow and develop. It is a huge support to have trusted people around who will also hold your feet to the fire. And Alan is the best business partner, friend and father.

Allen: Even with all the kids and business responsibilities, we find a way to get away for a weekend. If we are not home for a weekend, they will be just fine. We think it's healthy to do that. We also promote each other's individual friendships. I go on football weekends; she goes to the beach with all her friends. We don't ask for permission. We also think it's healthy to have and enjoy friendships outside of the marriage that enhance the marriage. I don't know how we fit it all into our calendar, but we do!

Theresa: We are both independent, confident people. I don't think either of us would do very well with a needy person. We believe in each person creating their own life, and it's true with our kids too. We don't have to be the only adults in their lives. Once I told Alan I needed to go to Idaho. I took four kids and went away for a month and said, "See ya." It was really good for us. He had a great time by himself. Everyone was happy. It was a vacation for him and a great time for me, too.

Allen: There were times when I had the kids and people would question Theresa. "How could you let a man take care of all these kids? Where is the mother figure?" We don't have defined roles — we can each be with our kids, alone or together, and have a great time. Our kids see that too. They don't need both of us to be around all the time.

Theresa: Whatever needs to be done, whether it's the business, the household, the children, whoever is around does it. We are interchangeable. A friend asked me, "How do you get your husband to do the vacuuming?!" The running joke is about what I don't do. I don't do the laundry, grocery shopping, cooking… at the office I don't pay the bills. So what do I do?!

Allen: I'll do the cooking, grocery shopping with the boys. It doesn't feel unusual to us. We both are very busy and yet know when and how to take time off to pick kids up or go to the pool. I can work later on my computer. The flexibility we have we give to our family and, in doing so, we take care of each other.

For **Peggy Burns and Richard Tubman** [p. 42] family is an ever-present support. When asked about support and caring for themselves, their children and their business, Peggy and Richard, the parents of two young adults, speak about their friends and their families.

Peggy: We have great friends from our time at college and those are still some of our closest friends. We have known them for 35 years and see them regularly. I have great girlfriends. We bike, go to the gym and travel together. And we have a lot of family — eleven siblings to begin with — some are local and others live in other states. Richard lucked out when he married me. We have a close family and we do a lot of things together. They are all very supportive. Often we host events here in our house. We've had 45 people here in 4 days, starting with a Seder, then a party, a celebration and ending with Easter dinner.

Richard: Today I see couples with young children struggling with finding babysitters. When our kids were young, they would stay with one of the grandmothers, or a cousin, an aunt. That was incredibly supportive and very different from babysitting.

Peggy: My sister Judy took care of the kids when we worked on Saturday. She was like an aunt, a grandmother and a mother. We have a Memorial Day sale at our warehouse, a feeding frenzy for one day. We call in the family — brothers, sisters, cousins, friends — all come in for the day. We have a barbeque and give out hot dogs and hamburgers, and do face painting. It's fun for everyone.

Richard: My becoming part of Peggy's family redefined the size and nature of family for me. It was very different from what I knew before.

Peggy: We hang out with our nieces and nephews in their thirties and forties who have kids, and have become close with them. Our kids like to hang out with us, too. A sense of family was inspired by my mother, who raised us on her own. Mom was my support and inspiration. She was very hardworking and the driving force in our lives. We could be down and out, and she would say, "Whatever you want to do, you can do it if you work hard." When everything was falling apart, she'd say, "You only have to make it through the next day." She wanted the best for us. As a kid I would only think of myself and feel miserable. She gave me perspective and made me want to do better. Mom didn't want material things. She wanted her kids to recognize that we had each other and to do well, and she wanted to be with her grandchildren.

The Next Generation

The next generation offers us the chance to have fun while contributing our love and care to our children's children. Grandparenting brings satisfaction of a different sort for **Lynne and Bill Twist** [p. 23].

Lynne: We're really good grandparents. We have four grandchildren, and we see them every week for two or three days. We sort of co-raise them from time to time. Bill is funny and fun and he'll wrestle with the kids, and they just adore him.

Miriam: Our grandchildren inspire us to care for ourselves as we care for them. We want to enjoy them as long as we can. They are our future and a powerful reason to care for all that is important to us. For example, when our granddaughter Callie labeled us "the adventure grandparents," we got to design adventures each summer with her and her sister. Camping and hiking and enjoying the outdoors was important to us growing up. For many years now we have shared those experiences with our granddaughters and created memories that will hopefully last their whole lifetime.

Our Perspective on Play and Re-creation

This chapter has offered you a chance to reflect on how you integrate — or separate — care for yourself and your relationship and care for the business. How do you balance work and play, blend these worlds together or separate them? Time spent on vacation brings you pleasure and enjoyment and nourishes you in substantially different ways from time spent on work and business development.

From our own experience and from conversations with many couples, we feel it is essential to cultivate practices that give you the "time out" to sustain yourself and your relationship while fulfilling your long-term commitment to your business. To have the energy to care for others, we must care for ourselves first. Developing a positive and proactive approach to self care supports our long term health and well-being and models that possibility for others — at home and at work.

Chapter Takeaways

1. Discuss your three favorite ways or experiences of caring for yourself and your relationship and how you can expand them.

2. Describe to your partner an area of self-care that you want to explore further: daily practices, play and vacations, passion and intimacy or recreation with family, friends, faith and the next generation.

3. With a partner, commit to an action or series of actions that you will take to make your answer to #2 a reality.

4. When the day is over, assess how you have cared for yourself and your relationship that day.

5. When the business quarter is complete, ask what element of self care have you sacrificed that you want to reaffirm or reintegrate? Discuss this with your partner.

Thoughts on this Chapter

_____

_____

_____

_____

_____

_____

_____

_____

_____

_____

_____

_____

_____

_____

_____

_____

_____

_____

_____

"Where there is great love, there are always miracles."

—WILLA CATHER (1873–1947)
AMERICAN NOVELIST

CHAPTER SIX

SOUL SUPPORT: ENCOURAGING EACH OTHER'S TALENTS AND GROWTH

T HIS CHAPTER IS DEDICATED TO the special qualities in every couple and in each individual.

*"We are all moved by greatness when we see it ... It is as
if something in us stirs, awakens, and comes forth to meet
what was inside us all along. When we respond to someone else's mag-
nificence, we feed our own. ...We cannot lose when we recognize that the
positive qualities we see in others belong also to us. Our recognition of
this is a call to action that, if heeded, will inspire others to see in us what
they also possess. This creates a chain reaction unfolding itself endlessly
into the future.*

*"Ultimately, what this soul support and encouragement of each other
brings forth is simply the best of what humanity has to offer... When we
see generosity of spirit, empathy and a commitment to excellence in others,
we know it, and when we trust its presence in ourselves, we embody it."*

—The Daily Om

Do you have a clear sense of how you contribute to each other's growth
in your partnership and to each other's leadership roles in the world? Do
you regularly give thought to how grateful you are for your partner? Do
you acknowledge her or his contributions to the relationship and the business? Do you also acknowledge *yourself*?

Providing soul support to your partner means consciously creating
a viewpoint from which you see the other person as an extraordinary
human being. This viewpoint is not true or false. It is a view beyond

just loving the other person; it is a view that always keeps them in your thoughts and spirit as being and doing their best in any situation. We experience being grateful simply for their being a part of our lives.

Here are some of the best examples of couples standing for each other that we extracted from our interviews.

Wynn and Douglas Waggoner [p. 88] were the first couple among those we interviewed who gave voice to the idea of creating an extraordinary relationship by contributing to each other's greatness.

Wynn: The support from him is just extraordinary; it's very different from how I grew up. That same permission to be myself occurs in the business part of the relationship as well as the personal part. It allows me to trust myself. It also keeps us in motion and doesn't allow anything to get stale.

Douglas: Wynn stands for my continued spiritual, mental and just overall human development in all areas of life. It's not that I expect it; that's just who she is for me. That kind of support gives me the space to be the best I can be. We can be with each other in a way that was nonexistent in any prior relationship, and it's all because of what we have generated for one another.

Matthew and Terces Engelhart [p. 91] have been married for nine years. They expressed a remarkable commitment to mutual support in both being great and having great lives.

Matthew: We made a deal in our relationship: she doesn't worry about her life anymore, she only worries about my life, while I take care of her life and I don't worry about my life anymore. She makes sure my life is great, and I make sure her life is great. So we've kind of given up managing our own lives, and it really works much better. We all get distracted when it becomes about, "Am I getting the love I want, am I getting the comfort I want?" That's a very small "me, me, me" game. I make sure her life is extraordinary, I make sure she feels beautiful and acknowledged and loved, and she does the same for me. So that's what we've taken on, and we each really keep up our end of the bargain.

What Greatness Looks Like

Values are deeply imbedded within every action we take. In addition to a vision and purpose for their business, the following couples experience a source of inspiration that extends beyond their relationship. This motivation fuels the vision for their individual and collective excellence in their business and in their lives, playing a central role in guiding and directing how they choose to actualize their vision.

Led by their dreams and values, **Anne and Christopher Ellinger** [p. 19] have an impressive background as philanthropic and wealth counselors, as well as organizers in the worldwide practice of Playback Theatre. They believe that the values you care deeply about can be infused into your whole way of life.

Anne: We met in our early twenties at Movement for Social Change, a social change community in Philadelphia. This radicalizing experience caught us at that perfect time in our lives, when our core values were being set. The times were hopeful, too, as the lessons of the 60s were used to spark a lot of effective organizing in the 70s and 80s. This energized context profoundly shaped our relationship.

It doesn't really matter what business we're doing. Our relationship is dedicated to trying to help this world, however you want to phrase it: to make it through these unbelievable crisis times, to transform consciousness, to create a more just and sustainable world. This core purpose is always there in our relationship.

Just this morning, thinking about the upcoming interview with you, we asked ourselves, "What difference do we think we've made?" Honestly, we know that we've had impact by just being who we are. There's a lot of despair about marriages not lasting, so our relationship gives people hope. People also struggle with feeling isolated, so the way we've built neighborhood community here is a piece of our work, as is living somewhat simply, putting meaningful work rather than making money at the core of our lives. Our love and our community building affect people. A vision guides our life and our relationship, and business is just one manifestation of that vision.

Rich and Antra Borofsky [p. 96], who have been together for 41 years, have a strong vision for being together and working together as a couple.

Antra: I met Rich at a professional meeting. I saw him across the room, and I was drawn to the warmth in his eyes.

Rich: This being 1970, the meeting began with an ice-breaker exercise. We were invited to pick a stranger and gaze into each other's eyes for ten minutes! I had noticed Antra from the moment I arrived. She seemed alluring and mysterious to me and I quickly contrived to partner with her.

Antra: And so did I! It was wonderful.

Rich: That was our first meeting — our first date.

Antra: It was an auspicious beginning, and we can't help but notice that we continue to gaze into each other's eyes — every day.

Rich: Our business is teaching and learning. We have learned how to sustain our loving connection and our work is to teach others how to do this. We're lovers at large!

Antra: We are artists of intimacy, and the process is subtle. Our strength is that we can very precisely articulate what isn't present in a relationship and what needs to happen in the moment to help it really blossom.

Rich: We are able to teach couples how to consciously practice strengthening and sustaining their connection. We can do this because we have learned through trial and error how to do it ourselves. Our main qualification for being teachers is that we love to learn.

Antra: An important part of the learning process is experimenting with different ways of making contact and observing what does and doesn't work. We have tried a lot of things that didn't work. Fortunately, we were persistent and creative enough to also find many things that did work, for us and for others.

Rich: The heart of what we have learned is that love is renewed and sustained by contact and requires continual maintenance. Love must become more resilient, robust, precise, wise and compassionate — or it will inevitably die.

"Presencing" Greatness: Gratitude, Acknowledgement, Trust

Often we cannot control what happens or how things unfold. What we *can* always control is the way we view an experience and how we respond to it. Holding a viewpoint of your partner as a great person allows you to tap into your creative abilities and gives you enormous power and leverage in life. You can ask your partner, "How can I contribute to your greatness today?" You can hold that intention even if you don't ask the question, don't get a specific response or are upset with your partner. It helps to have a perspective of gratitude and a practice of acknowledgement.

Gratitude

"Gratitude unlocks the fullness of life. It turns what we have into enough, and more. It turns denial into acceptance, chaos into order, confusion into clarity... It turns problems into gifts, failures into success, the unexpected into perfect timing, and mistakes into important events. Gratitude makes sense of our past, brings peace for today and creates a vision for tomorrow." [1]

Gratitude is the experience of being deeply, warmly aware of benefits given and received. Gratitude can easily lead to acknowledgement — expressions of gratitude spoken, conveyed affectionately in word or action, or given as a gift. Acknowledgement is recognizing and expressing another person's actions that made a difference, a thoughtful recognition of another's contribution.

Early on in our lives, our parents, teachers and other significant caretakers teach us whether and how to express our feelings. You may feel gratitude and yet have grown up in a family or culture where the custom was to not show your appreciation overtly. Even if you weren't encouraged and supported in this as a child, as an adult you can still develop a regular practice of acknowledging the small and large gifts of the people with whom you live and work.

"At times our own light goes out and is rekindled by a spark from another person. Each of us has cause to think with deep gratitude of those who have lighted the flame within us." [2]

"If the only prayer you said in your whole life was "Thank you," that would suffice." [3]

---

[1] Melody Beattie, *The Language of Letting Go*. (Center City, MN: Hazelden Foundation, 1990).
[2] Albert Schweitzer (1875 – 1965) philosopher, medical missionary, Nobel Peace Prize winner.
[3] Johannes "Meister" Eckhart, (c. 1260 – 1327) theologian, philosopher and mystic.

Acknowledgement

"All of the people in our lives are saints; it is just that some of them have day jobs and most will never have feast days named for them."[4]

By expressing gratitude to our partners we support the best in them, and can unleash their special qualities. There are many opportunities to acknowledge our partners for something they did, or for their way of being — such as listening carefully or responding lovingly — that make a difference in our experience. Even a small "thank you" can have a large impact on how we feel or think, and consequently on our relationships and our businesses.

When we are honest with ourselves, we know that project deadlines, family crises and momentary challenges distract us from pausing to acknowledge one another as often as we might. Successful couples reap the benefits of a genuine "thank you" in response to the small and large acts of cooperation, kindness and caring we show to one another daily.

Each of the couples we interviewed discovered effective ways to acknowledge each other and the contributions they make. In their interview, **Matthew and Terces Engelhart** [p. 91] gave wonderful examples of generous appreciation.

Matthew: Yes, she's a Virgo, so her thing is detail, detail, detail — way more than me. I'm a Gemini, so my thing is communication, keeping everyone on board. I love to talk about the numbers, but I don't really want to do anything to make sure the numbers are right. In my previous business, I had no interest in systems, so I paid people to do it. Terces brings hard work and creativity, like an amazing chef. She also brings a lot of love, and people love to work with her; she makes sure that the people around her are in great shape.

Terces: I would say that Matthew's strengths are his endless ability to be available for people. People walk in and he can just shift his attention from one person to another; he seems to have an endless ability to be a resource for people in an extraordinary way. He has an expansive vision that encompasses more, and so he's willing to go for whatever, to keep playing a bigger and bigger game. He's so lighthearted, fine and happy to be around.

---

[4]Robert Benson, *Between the Dreaming and the Coming True: The Road Home to God.* (San Francisco: HarperSanFrancisco, 1996).

Although he doesn't see himself as good at dealing with details, he's very good at dealing with specifics about people. For example, he can remember where somebody was born, where they lived, what their kids' names were, where he saw them last — those kinds of things. That ability makes people feel really appreciated and recognized. I think that's extraordinary.

He's also really good at pushing the envelope; by that I mean he doesn't let people stay in their individual view. He's always asking them to see something way beyond that. That's part of having a big vision that he brings to both our relationship and the business. He brings an unwavering commitment to the relationship, to me and my well-being, making sure that my life's great, that our children's lives are great. I don't ever question that, and I never have to worry about it.

Also, he is very attentive to the balance in our lives. I could just work and work and work, and it's not a problem for me; I love it, I enjoy it. But he makes sure that we get to yoga, that we get massages, and that we get to Hawaii.

Matthew: I'm on the fun committee.

Interviewer: Seems like you're chairman of it!

Matthew: Definitely. There are many challenges, and we both have moments of "something's wrong." It's the greatest thing about being a couple in business. When she's challenged by the circumstances, I'm seeing the opportunity, and vice versa. So you're always lifting each other up.

The Bond of Trust

At the heart of each couple's greatness is a bond of trust. This same bond rests at the core of choosing to be a couple in business. People who want to work closely in partnership must be committed to learning how to trust each other. When you're in business together, you can't walk away and blame someone or something else, for example, the economy. In order to resolve any and all issues that can help ensure your financial and emotional well-being, you must face each other and find ways to resolve these issues.

Trust doesn't always come naturally. Some members of the couples we interviewed grew up in successful business families that demonstrated the importance of trust. Others chose to participate in seminars and programs where they received the kind of coaching that allowed them to understand how essential trust is to their success.

This bond remains central whether you as a couple are married, gay or straight, and whether you choose to divorce and continue as business partners. You still can support each other's strengths and enjoy each other's company.

Jessica Lipnack and Jeffrey Stamps [p. 62] talk about a concept of "the bond" based on the work of Virginia Hine, an anthropologist who co-authored a number of books and a very famous paper on networks.

Jeffrey: Virginia Hine spoke about the bond, not just between a married couple, but a bond in any partnership that is truly synergistic, tight and enduring. She believed that that bond was at the heart of all human organizations of any scale and any size.

Part of exploring the bond has been trying to understand what an organization is but, even more fundamentally, what an "us" is and what a "we" is. That does start with two because that's the smallest "us" and the smallest "we." Every larger "we" is always made up of pairs, one way or another. Whether we're enduring pairs or transactional pairs, it always takes two to tango. There's still something kind of magical, unreachable and unfathomable at the core of what the bond is — it goes to the heart of who we are and what we're trying to accomplish.

Deepening Trust and Meeting the Challenge

Trust and partnership are not givens — they are creations that we bring into our lives together, ever more deeply over time. Learning to stay connected while managing family and business life is a challenge that requires a loving, trusting relationship ... and at the same time deepens that relationship, that sense of "us," as this next couple illustrates.

PHILIP CASS AND LAURA WEISEL

Phil Cass (62) and Laura Weisel (62) are a co-executive couple from Columbus, Ohio. They met more than 25 years ago as leaders with shared professional concerns for mental health services and leadership development. For their entire professional lives they have each worked to provide services to underserved populations, including people with mental illnesses, the uninsured, struggling learners, and individuals who have difficulties with sustainable employment. Laura started her business, The TLP Group, 17 years ago, researching and developing transformational systems and products for organizations serving people with literacy and learning challenges. Phil is currently the CEO of the Columbus Medical Association and affiliates. They married eleven years ago, a second marriage for both, and have four grown children between them.

Phil and Laura speak about their vision for their personal relationship and where they are on the journey toward achieving it.

Laura: I think we're constantly creating our vision of the relationship and it's challenging to do. We are in the midst of figuring out how we are going to stay happily connected during this phase, in the next phase in our lives, and in the life of our family.

Phil: In my previous marriage, I created tension around the conflict between work and family life, and the marriage ended up not working. In this relationship, I am free of that tension. There is respect for each other's work, and I feel Laura's love and support. But sometimes I can still not pay enough attention to our personal relationship. I think we're still very much in the process of developing what "us" is.

Laura: I don't think either of us saw a role model in our families for what this kind of partnership could look like. I saw clearly what hard work was all about; my father was an entrepreneur, so I certainly understood the effort, pleasure and pride in ownership. Yet I never saw the slowing down to nurture the primary relationship. That's something Phil and I are learning and practicing together.

Creating the Other's Greatness

"What we see depends mainly on what we look for."

— *John Lubbock*

In our intimate relationships and in our business relationships, we regularly alter our viewpoint of one another and our vision of what's possible. Choosing to see somebody as "great" is a viewpoint you can take on and, at any moment, you can commit to having a new experience of the other. Choice is the key.

Choosing a viewpoint that makes you active champions for each other's success is a commitment to achievement exemplified by **Alina and Ron Chand** [p. 44].

Alina: Ron has brought out the strength in me to reach for things that I may not have tried to reach for on my own. I was always a confident person. I liked myself, and felt I could do a lot, but only to a certain level. Ron made me see that I can go higher, try even harder and perform at my highest level. I'd say, "I don't want to do it," and he would encourage me, saying, "Listen, if you can't do it, nobody can." He gave me the push to go to the next level, and I discovered that I can do really well there.

This viewpoint, obviously, is easier to take when you feel loving and connected than when you feel distant and angry. The real test of your own character is your ability to choose the viewpoint or vision of the other's greatness when you feel small, angry and hurt by your partner's behavior, whether at home or at work. That is when your commitment to each other's greatness is strongly tested and when it matters the most.

We had an experience in our own relationship that illustrates this point. It involved Jeffrey's actively choosing to see Miriam as greater than her momentary reactions.

Jeffrey: One day, on a drive to Cape Cod, Massachusetts to work on this book, we had a fight. The content of the fight is not all that interesting. In fact, it was pretty repetitive and boring, as many fights are for most couples. Much more important was that no matter how angry I was about Miriam's actions, I was able to take two actions that made a difference.

One was to accept Miriam for who she is and who she isn't and see her as a person who is greater than her behavior at that time. The other was seeing our relationship as greater than both of us. The power of seeing the relationship this way opened a forgiving space in my heart and allowed me to feel free to love her. That love superseded her limitations and transformed my own experience of this petty argument. What I also discovered once again is that if you don't add fuel to the fire, it will soon burn out on its own.

The power to choose was so important to this next couple that they included it in three new promises for their union when, at a crisis point in their relationship, they renewed their vows. These promises inspire them — and us.

KATHARINE AND ALAN CAHN

Katharine (58) and Alan (61) Cahn are a co-professional couple living in Portland, Oregon. Alan is a senior program leader with an international educational company which provides training and development in effectiveness for individuals and organizations. Katharine has three intersecting roles as professor, social worker and executive director. Their marriage began in 1979, and in 1998 they renewed their vows. Now married for 32 years, they are the parents of two grown children, Rael (37) and Rose (31), also married. In all aspects of their lives, Alan and Katharine have vowed to be of service and to make a difference in the lives of every person they touch.

Alan: Our first promise is to be the source of our relationship. The second promise is to love each other, always. And then here's the toughest one...

Katharine: This one is pretty impossible.

Alan: This one will keep us for a lifetime. We promise to be empowered by however the other person is being. Yes, that's the biggest challenge.

You can choose to see your partner as greater than his or her habits and reactions. And you can be empowered by however he or she is being, as the Cahns invite us to do.

Our Perspective on Greatness

You have a smile on your face. You are looking lovingly at your partner. His or her support has just opened up a new business opportunity for you both, and he or she has just acknowledged you for your contribution. You feel great. Your body is relaxed and your heart is open, not just to your partner, but to the whole world. This is the transformed state we have been talking about in this chapter, where it is possible to be the best you can be in your relationship and your business.

> *"The foundation of greatness is honoring the small things of the present moment, instead of pursuing the idea of greatness."*
>
> — *Eckhart Tolle*

Chapter Takeaways

1. Identify the talents and qualities you include in your partner's greatness and your own.

2. Select one new action or practice that will support you and your partner's greatness and tell them.

3. Express to your partner what you are grateful for today.

4. Appreciate and acknowledge three things about yourself and your partner today.

5. Notice what fresh thoughts, new insights and possibilities are opening up for you as a result of this exploration, and let your partner know.

Thoughts on this Chapter

_____

_____

_____

_____

_____

_____

_____

_____

_____

_____

_____

_____

_____

_____

_____

_____

_____

_____

*"When we quit thinking primarily about ourselves
and our own self-preservation, we undergo
a truly heroic transformation of consciousness."*

—JOSEPH CAMPBELL (1904–1987)
AMERICAN MYTHOLOGIST, WRITER AND PHILOSOPHER

CHAPTER SEVEN

NO BARRIERS: PARTNERSHIPS WITH LOCAL AND GLOBAL IMPACT

"To belong to a community is to act as a creator and co-owner of that community."

— *Peter Block, author of* Community:
The Structure of Belonging, *2008.*

I N THIS CHAPTER WE DISCUSS the value of service in the context of community. As human beings, we exist in relationship to a world of other people. Our lives are interwoven with our intimate others, our friends and closest relations, with our colleagues, our neighbors and others we meet throughout our day. We are also connected with many people we may not know personally. Ultimately, we live in towns, in cities, in countries, and we all belong to the global community of Earth.

Many couples in business are actively engaged in contributing thought, time and money through their various communities of interest, whether secular or religious. In fact, many design their lives and businesses for the express purpose of making a difference in the world around them.

As you work to create, establish and expand the reach of your relationship and your business, you will naturally look for opportunities to contribute to your communities, to be of service and to make a difference in the world. In turn the communities you choose to be a part of will make a difference in your life. How *do* the communities you choose to be part of make a difference in your life? Through your participation in community, you contribute to creating a world that is sustainable, just and peaceful for yourself, for your generation and for the generations to come. Fully participating and following through on your promises will make all the difference.

Visions for Making a Contribution to Your Communities

Some individuals are compelled by a vision of contribution. From their first meeting, this couple shared a commitment to community and to making a difference in the world.

PETER KEVORKIAN AND PATTI GIULIANO

Peter Kevorkian (54) and Patti Giuliano (58) have been a couple for 28 years. Both attended chiropractic school, and they met in 1983 at a conference in Boston. They fell in love over lunch even though Patti was engaged to someone else. They married five months later with a commitment to practice together. They now have a thriving practice, Westwood Family Chiropractic, in Massachusetts. Their two grown children are Christopher (22) and Kathryn (24).

Peter: Our vision from day one was to improve the world in any way that we possibly could.

Patti: We fell in love with each other largely because we look at the world in the same way. We were both chiropractors and had a vision for chiropractic that fit in with our life visions.

Peter: The roots of our vision are philosophical. Personally, the philosophy of our profession drives me. What drew us together was a level of congruency and shared philosophy. Our vision for our business and our life is one and the same. For us, chiropractic is as much what happens at the dinner table as what happens on an adjusting table. It's just as much a part of our communication, no matter where we are or what we're doing.

Patti: It's not like I have a personal face and a professional face. This is it: this is me, this is my life, and if there is anything you want to know, ask away!

Peter: The essence of our profession honors the fact that there is order in the universe… everything that happens around us is part of how this universe is pieced together. Suffice it to say that if you believe everything has a purpose, then you don't need to view anything as wrong.

Patti: When someone comes to our practice for help with a symptom, we understand that symptom is a reflection of something that needs attention, something that needs to be honored and appreciated for what it is. It's a communication of information from the body.

Our service is, first, to clinically address problems within the spine and nervous system that may be interfering with a person's healing or contributing to their symptoms; and second, we want to help our patients develop or deepen their own awareness of the need for improved self care.

Peter: The same is true for our lives. We believe that everything that happens to us in our relationship — with our kids, in our house, with our friends — is an opportunity for discovery and learning.

Our vision is to build the awareness in other people that there is a beautiful intelligence that guides and drives our bodies. It's a genius inside, and the greatest thing you can do is connect with that — learn from it, embrace it, allow it to be your teacher, your healer. Instead of fixing anything, we are trying to make people aware of interferences with the plan. That is what happens in our practice. It's akin to helping people understand that the world is round.

Patti: The same things are in play in our relationship. I believe every relationship should be one of joy and ecstasy as well as accepting and calmly facing areas of anxiety, sorrow and upset — in other words, rather than resisting, accepting and allowing the full expression, the full dance of life. This is our contribution to each other and to all others.

Being of Service

Being of service is a core value for most of the couples you have encountered in this book. **Katharine and Alan Cahn** [p. 135] consciously created their relationship to be of service; they articulate the goal of an "outward facing relationship," which is one that places the highest value on service and connection to the world.

Katharine: We got married before we had all of the distinctions and language we have now or the kind of coaching we've had since. But even when we were young we were both really clear that the reason to be related to each other wasn't about the relationship. The relationship would be a foundation for the difference that we wanted to make in the world. So when we got married we stood together, lit a candle and said to the people who were assembled that both of us were totally clear that our life together was about being of service. That our marriage would be another vehicle for my vision — service. And I could see that with Alan's past as well. We don't have an inward-facing relationship. We have an outward-facing relationship, where we joined together as companions to empower each other to be of service in the world.

Another way to be of service is to use your professional skills to help others feel good about themselves regardless of their life circumstances. In his work as a makeup artist and entrepreneur **David Nicholas** [p. 48] has a guiding vision for developing his own product line.

David: Well, it may sound cliché, but it really is to help people. One of my biggest jobs is my reconstructive, corrective work. I deal with people going through many difficult life transitions. I deal with women who are obese, and with cross-dressers and transgenders, both pre- and post-operative. Also, when you are with somebody who's dying, they want to feel better about saying good-bye to those they love and not look like the disease has ravaged them.

The opportunity to contribute to people in these conditions and circumstances is what keeps me going. I love the worlds of beauty, fashion and theatre, yet I couldn't just do that. And I don't think I could just do the other either. It would get a little too intense. The combination is what allows each to flourish. Also, because this is so complex, it requires two of us working full-time as a team. Since we've been married, we've also been on a mission to illustrate the healthful benefits of couple relationships. So we're partaking in a lot of things that maybe we normally wouldn't have, which is why this interview seemed to be appropriate, very well timed, and I think is going to help people.

We can clearly each make a difference, one person or one family at a time, one business at a time, and likewise impact big global efforts. **Dorothy and Wayne Stingley** [p. 76] have used their multiple McDonald's businesses to accomplish all three: first, to provide higher education for Wayne's children, secondly to inspire other black business owners, and thirdly to contribute to organizations addressing health and world hunger.

Dorothy: I weaseled my way in and became valuable to the business. We now own and operate eleven McDonald's restaurants. We grew that business from one restaurant to two to three. In 1993 we relocated to Arizona to acquire number four, and then we grew to nine. In 2007 we added number ten, and number eleven in 2008. They are now all in Arizona, within fifteen miles of each other.

Having great business success enables you to give more support in terms of time and money to the organizations whose work or mission you want to support. Dorothy and Wayne speak about their contributions to community.

Dorothy: Wayne started the business. He came out of a nineteen-year career teaching high school. His vision was to afford to send his kids to college. He had five kids when I started working with him. Now that all but one of our children are adults, and four of the seven have college degrees, we've transformed the vision of our business. We are now operating the business to make a difference in the world beyond the scope of caring for the needs of our family. We are continuing to grow our business and our wealth so that we can be philanthropic. We are committed to fostering self-reliance and opportunity for all people. We fund scholarships, we sponsor a Teach for America teacher, and we help fund the global work of The Hunger Project.

Wayne: We also participate in the Ronald McDonald House, which is a charitable organization started by the Philadelphia Eagles, and one of the charities in which we love to participate. It began when one player's child had to be hospitalized. They discovered that oftentimes couples don't have the means to stick around the hospital while their child is being attended to medically. Out of that grew the Ronald house, McDonald's way of giving something back to the community. For years I wasn't too interested because I was involved with The Hunger Project, but I was introduced to it after I got involved with McDonald's, and I saw a lot of similarities. One of my favorite quotes is "the tide raises all boats." It just stands to reason that whatever you can do for anybody anywhere contributes to everyone everywhere. It has a trickle down or multiplying effect. I believe that when somebody's life is improved everybody's life is improved.

Dorothy: The emerging vision for the last few years has involved some of our McDonald's business partners joining us in The Hunger Project and our joining them in other philanthropic initiatives, linking our identity as McDonald's owner/operators and entrepreneurs with our philanthropy. The aim is business philanthropy, as distinct from non-business philanthropy.

Wayne: We were hiding out. We would write you a check in secret but we would not want to be known for it or identified with it.

Dorothy: So we've come out. We are proud of the part we have played in the evolution of the current global McDonald's business organization. We have become a very diverse community worldwide.

Interviewer: When was your "coming out"?

Dorothy: About five years ago — I initiated it because I represented the charter investors of The Hunger Project. So in front of a room of about 1,500 people, I announced to everyone what it was like to invest $100,000 or more a year in the work of The Hunger Project. Then Wayne raised some funds for a capital campaign for the local Ronald McDonald House — our second house here. He was recognized by the operator community with the Ronald award, which is given to one owner operator in each region each year. We also received the Gerry Newman McTLC Award, which comes with a $50,000 grant to the charity of our choice, highlighting our work in the community.

Interviewer: Congratulations!

Dorothy: This gives us a powerful context within which to be related. Some couples are related to their communities through raising their children, through creating family, or as business partners. We are related in all those ways, but the larger context for all that is making a difference and being global citizens.

Wayne: Our experience is that if you have a really big game to play, all those things — raising your kids, having your family work and your business work — get taken care of in the context of the bigger picture. You simply have to handle those things or you'll never get to the bigger picture.

Creativity and Shifting Community Consciousness
In the course of our interviews, we met couples who also enjoyed contributing through their creativity with books, games, retreats, food and much more.

Matthew and Terces Engelhart [p. 91] use these very vehicles to transform people's awareness from the individual to a more collective point of view. Their products and their businesses are beautiful examples of the shift toward community consciousness in action.

Matthew: We have this idea of shifting human consciousness from scarcity, which we're all caught up in — as in there's not enough love, not enough money, not enough time — to a view of a world as a place of abundance. That's a big game, and everything we do is informed by that game. What is it going to take for human consciousness to get out of this sleep state of not enough? Clearly there's enough. The evidence is that there's plenty, but people still say that there's not enough. That's what informs our everyday decisions and choices. That's what I mean by creating a context to support the view that there is enough for all.

Alan and Katharine Cahn [p. 135] see their own relationship as opening up possibilities for countless others.

Alan: Inside our relationship we are creating the option of possibilities for all people. Part of my vision is that our relationship is dynamic, expanding, exciting, never static and always there. Because we come into contact with so many people, my intention is that our relationship kindles in people the idea of what relationships can be. Personally and professionally I have the same vision: to have a world where the power and magic of transformation is alive and real for everyone.

Building Community from Generation to Generation
The significance of community is highlighted in the pleasure of entertaining others, traveling together, and joyously celebrating all kinds of occasions. What is important, in addition to having a good time, is the building and nurturing of communities that can support the kind of life we want to live.

Miriam: In Jeffrey's and my life together, we have celebrated Passover for more than 30 years with a group of women from *Our Bodies, Ourselves*, along with their partners. For most of these gatherings, four generations have been present at the Seder. Babies have been born, and successive generations have taken the initiative in organizing the event. At the beginning of each Seder, we as a group honor members of the community and of our extended families who have died. We use stories and humorous vignettes to enhance the continuity of the community.

Global Citizens in Action
Many of the couples we interviewed continue to have a far-reaching impact on present generations. Some, like **Suzanne and Dwight Frindt** [p. 18], actively plan for their impact on future generations.

The Frindts named their business "2130 Partners" to express the company's core philosophy that "leaders are accountable in their decision making for their impact on each of the next seven generations." They estimated that seven generations would bring them to the year 2130 — in other words, 140 years from the company's inception in 1990, which was the beginning of their commitment to work from a long-term, vision-focused perspective. This is how they are looking out for generations of community.

Some of our couples travel widely and have direct personal influence in the international arena, using their relationships and their businesses to extend their reach as global citizens and make a difference for the world.

Petra Krauledat and Peter Hansen [p. 77] share a global vision for the health and well-being of all people. Their fourth business in the field of medical technology is distinct from all the others.

Petra: It was a mission that others encouraged us to take on — being able to develop the technology to do AIDS diagnostics and AIDS monitoring in Africa. We had been involved in such technology off and on, and others who recognized our experience asked us to come up with a design that could work in the developing world. We needed to create something more sophisticated that could make up for the shortage of educated people to monitor the technology.

Peter: We think we are solving the problem of getting antiretroviral drugs into the hands of the people who need them. If you simply give the drugs to people based on the appearance of the person's signs and symptoms, you have a 20% efficacy rate with the drugs. If, however, you actually take a blood cell count during the course of the patient's specific HIV progression, there is a certain cell count that is a direct one-to-one signal of the immune status of that patient. There is an optimum time to begin giving the drugs. So having the ability to do this cell count is the biggest deal in being able to roll out the drugs. The issue is, how do you get this cell counting facility out in a country with little infrastructure? That is what our company is about.

Petra: For instance, there is a dramatic need for malaria testing and better methods for TB testing. I could go on. These are greatly underserved and problematic areas for the general development of Africa, India and a number of other countries. The overall vision for the business is not to stop with the AIDS crisis but to continue to develop additional products that simply improve health care for people who don't live in the

U.S., Japan, Australia or Europe. What's important for this to occur is to carefully analyze their lifestyles, their way of life, and not to assume that what's good in America and Europe is what they need or want. That's just not the case.

Philip and Katy Leakey [p. 27] are another couple with deep ties to Africa, and a commitment to "building a bridge of understanding between Africa and the West." They developed a way for Maasai women, already experienced in making beautiful beadwork, to use native grasses, clay and other materials to create beads for necklaces and other jewelry that is now sold in boutiques around the world.

Philip: When we came together and married, we were both determined to work together. We didn't see any point in getting married and going in different directions, so it was important to find opportunities that kept us together on a daily basis. In this particular business, we were able to complement each other on just about everything. We also made a decision that we would only do things that worked for both of us, and the business seemed to satisfy that requirement. We both enjoy people and supporting their welfare and success. We also both enjoy being creative, and love the lifestyle we have out in the bush in Kenya.

Katy: The long-term vision for the company suits our desires, not only in business but also in what we want to leave behind. For instance, both of us have been interested in building a bridge of understanding between Africa and the West, and this business certainly does that. As for the vision of the future, we see this company as a lifestyle company.

In addition to products, there are other facets, like education. For example, we plan to work with The Wharton School at the University of Pennsylvania to bring our brand of training to a business school. We will also be getting into research and development in rural enterprise. We can pass that on to the people of Kenya and develop more models for working with raw materials and for training people in other areas and climates. It's a long process that will keep expanding, and we both love that!

Both of our families have been very involved in public service. We decided we didn't want to just make widgets, but rather we wanted to create something that would have a life long after ours. That was a conscious choice, one that is at the heart of what we do in our business.

Philip: We both love nature. We believe there is enormous potential for businesses to emerge out of natural products and the sustainable development of rural areas and natural resources. This business is a great fit with our backgrounds and with that understanding. I've always made my living from natural products in one way or another. And we both have always been involved with many groups of people. Our individual backgrounds have merged to create what we collectively do now.

Celebrating Latin Culture Worldwide: More Bridge Builders
Rosi and Brian Amador [p. 108] are another pair of effective bridge builders. They created a Latin band that promotes and celebrates Latin culture through its music. Their complementary skills came together in caring for their family and for the world through their music.

Rosi: One of our strongest goals is to build cultural bridges and build hope through our songs. The songs are a combination of original material created primarily by Brian, with some influence from me, combined with contemporary and traditional composers. It's music we love!

Brian: Our girls feel like our band is their band. Several years ago, one of them wrote an essay, "This is about my band, Sol y Canto." They have a great relationship with all the musicians. They have toured and performed with us. Having kids was the final incentive that drove us to do a children's album.

Rosi: The girls were recorded on our last CD.

Brian: One of them in particular is as at home on stage as she is in our backyard. She's a natural performer like her Mommy. The other one also likes to perform although she's a little more reserved. The band is like an extension of their family. Recently, when we mentioned to the girls that we were discussing cutting back on the touring they said, "Oh no, that would be horrible because then we wouldn't get to go to all those places."

Rosi: "We wouldn't see all our friends!"

Brian: I said, "Maybe you could have a dog." Then they said, "Oh, okay!!"

Rosi: I am looking at how I can reshape my life to make myself less crazy, and make sure I am there to guide my children. They needed us when they were in middle school, and they need us even more now that they are in high school.

National and International Business Focused on Communal Contributions

While **Ron and Alina Chand's** [p. 44] business has an international reach, they are focused on the community in which they live, with an emphasis on making a difference in the world. Ron Chand personally thrives on his deep commitment to his customers *and* community.

Ron: Our business is international, but mostly national. It's a love relationship with the business community as well as the community in which we live. Because the whole idea for our business and our lives is based on being of service to make a better world we go the extra mile for our customers. It doesn't matter whether they are able to pay for it or not. If they can't pay for it, we just take what they are able to pay. We adjust prices. It is a wonderful relationship with customers and with the community as well. Alina and I have served on many non-profit boards locally, and contribute our time and resources wherever we can.

There's a story we heard from several couples whose career aspirations reinforced their desire to work together. Since both partners were career-oriented, in each case the couple realized that if they didn't work together their work would take them away from each other, which they felt would not be a good thing for their particular relationship. These couples knew they wanted to spend more time together, so why not work together? Once they realized how great it was, it became clear that their first choice would always be to keep working together.

The challenge of doing something "bigger" was also appealing. One couple said that if they didn't do something bigger than just live their "puny little lives," they would probably eventually get divorced because they wouldn't have anything big enough to make it worth it.

This couple's marriage was already fine. They had no reason to spend the rest of their lives working on their relationship — they had a great relationship. So they asked themselves, "Now what?" Out of that inquiry, they created a great business. That accomplished, the next question they asked each other was, "Now what?" That helped them decide to have children. Then they had a great relationship, a great business and a great family. Guess what they were asking themselves? Yup, "Now what?!" So they turned their attention to how they could make an even bigger difference in the world.

Our Perspective on Contribution

Our lives, — Miriam's and Jeffrey's — are dedicated to generating conversations that enhance the quality of life on all levels. Our hope is that this comes across for you, and that the four main motivators and the seven key elements that we have described and illustrated will make a difference in your conversations with one another and in how you plan your lives together. We firmly believe that it is possible for you to create a quality of life that is fresh and authentic, sufficient in the area of relationship, satisfying in the arenas of business and finance, and informed by your conscious choices.

The great George Bernard Shaw issued this call to experience life in all its fullness, wonder and joy:

> *"This is the true joy in life, the being used for a purpose recognized by yourself as a mighty one; the being a force of nature instead of a feverish, selfish little clod of ailments and grievances, complaining that the world will not devote itself to making you happy. I am of the opinion that my life belongs to the whole community, and as long as I live it is my privilege to do for it whatever I can. I want to be thoroughly used up when I die, for the harder I work, the more I live. I rejoice in life for its own sake. Life is no brief candle to me; it is a sort of splendid torch which I have got hold of for the moment, and I want to make it burn as brightly as possible before handing it on to future generations."*

Chapter Takeaways

1. Speak with your partner about your own experience of community.

2. Name community leaders and activists who have inspired your contributions.

3. Reflect on how your community contributions have influenced your business and your relationship.

4. Acknowledge the most meaningful contributions you have received and those you have made, individually and together.

5. Discuss what new challenges you are now inspired to take on.

Thoughts on this Chapter

_____

_____

_____

_____

_____

_____

_____

_____

_____

_____

_____

_____

_____

_____

_____

_____

_____

_____

"*I wanted a perfect ending. Now I've learned, the hard way, that some poems don't rhyme, and some stories don't have a clear beginning, middle, and end. Life is about not knowing, having to change, taking the moment and making the best of it, without knowing what's going to happen next. Delicious ambiguity.*"

—GILDA RADNER (1946–1989)
ACTRESS AND COMEDIAN

THE JOYS AND CHALLENGES OF GROWING YOUR BUSINESS TOGETHER—AN ORGANIC ART FORM THAT TAKES ON A LIFE OF ITS OWN

W E WOULD LIKE TO LEAVE you with some ideas that have emerged from our many years of working with couples in business together or planning to create that kind of partnership.

Like any creative entrepreneur, you as a business couple can begin with an idea and with the resources you now have — money, time, people, experience and reputation — and get into action. Take a step forward and see how you do. If that step is successful, you can take the next, then the next and so forth. All along the way you can reassess and change your strategy, or even your business, as some copreneurial couples choose to do.

As you've seen throughout these chapters, couples create businesses for both economic and lifestyle reasons. In an economy where jobs are scarce and unemployment is high, going into business as a couple may be the only attractive option for you, or it may simply feel less risky than the alternatives, such as staying in corporate jobs with no secure future, being out of work, or waiting for the next opportunity to arise.

As you get started in business, don't be timid: ask for help and support from family, friends and colleagues, and network in your communities. In the process of developing your business you will find yourself building more resilient connections and stronger ties to your various communities.

Lifestyle choice — the kind of life you want and how you want it to feel — often drives the decision to step into business together. Many of us want to be more present to our families, including our children and our parents, and want to enjoy spending as much time as we can with our partners or spouses. We also have dreams and life purposes that we want to fulfill. To fully express your values in business as well as in your home and community life you will need to make business choices that reflect those deeply held values. The clearer this intention and resolve are, the more they lead you to create a wonderful business together where your values can be expressed consistently in all arenas of your lives.

Being a couple who are in business together can require great sacrifice, risk and courage. But whether you choose to develop a large, robust enterprise or prefer to stay small — while also becoming profitable of course — you can create a work life that allows you to preserve your connection to family and community.

When you have the freedom to view business as a work of art that makes a profit and expresses values, your business choices will naturally allow room for growth, learning and improvement. The more you are in continual and committed communication with one another, the more you will be able to make the adjustments necessary for your relationship and business to flourish. Creative, flexible and entrepreneurial couples discover ways to be financially successful, certainly, and something more happens: they discover strategies, practices, processes and systems that enable relationship, family and community to coexist rather than compete for available resources.

Couples who create successful and enduring businesses operate within the context of *both/and* rather than *either/or*, and they create this same context and possibility for their employees. When you take on the challenge and commitment from this point of view you can successfully invent and reinvent ways to integrate business, family and relationship.

We live in a time when the world is calling for more vibrant businesses, more vital relationships, healthier families and more thriving communities. Embodying the principle of *both/and* allows us to access our resources to the fullest, and points the way for any business venture we undertake to serve its highest purpose.

Ultimately there is no one way, one ideal partnership, one final conclusion as to how you or I or any of us should live our lives. What does exist are limitless opportunities, and creating a partnership in business, as well as in love, with your life partner is one choice. It was one we made, and the one we continue to choose, as have many of the couples you met throughout the book. Hopefully this is a choice you now have full ammunition to intelligently consider, with the shared stories helping you create or improve your partnership in ways that successfully inform and satisfy every aspect of your lives and the lives of everyone with whom you come in contact. That is our hope for you, and our commitment to the common good.

Thank you for staying with us for this incredible journey, and please feel free to visit us online and share your own story with us for our next book.

Until then, we wish you the best of health, happiness and prosperity!

MIRIAM AND JEFFREY
CAMBRIDGE, MASS.

RESOURCES

ROSI AND BRIAN AMADOR

Rosi Amador
Brian Amador
Amador Bilingual Voiceovers & Sol y Canto
199 Pemberton Street
Cambridge, MA 02140
rosi@amadorbilingualvoiceovers.com
www.amadorbilingualvoiceovers.com
brian@musicamador.com
www.brianamadormusic.com
617-492-1515 (office)

MARK ANDRUS AND STACY MADISON

Mark Andrus
moandrus@yahoo.com
781-962-7347 (cell)

LESLIE AND RON ARSLANIAN

Leslie Arslanian
Ronald Arslanian
General Optical Company
2038 Massachusetts Avenue
Cambridge, MA 02140
leslie@generaloptical.com
ronalda@generaloptical.com
www.generaloptical.com
617-864-0204 (office)

LIZA ROESER ATWOOD AND BLU ATWOOD

Liza Roeser Atwood
Blu Atwood
FiftyFlowers.com
960 East Ojai, #105
Ojai, CA 93023

liza@FiftyFlowers.com
blu@FiftyFlowers.com
www.FiftyFlowers.com
805-646-4578 (office)

RICH AND ANTRA BOROFSKY

Rich Borofsky
Antra Borofsky
Center for the Study of Relationship
86 Washington Avenue
Cambridge, MA 02140
borofskys@borofsky.net
www.beingtogether.com
617-661-7890 (office)

PEGGY BURNS AND RICHARD TUBMAN

Peggy Burns
Richard Tubman
Circle Furniture
19 Craig Road
Acton, MA 01720
peggy@circlefurniture.com
rtubman@circlefurniture.com
www.circlefurniture.com
978-263-4509 (office)
339-222-2068 (cell - Peggy)
339-222-2076 (cell - Richard)

GINGER BURR AND MARION DAVIS

Ginger Burr
Total Image Consultants
14 Lewis Street
Lynn, MA 01902
ginger@totalimageconsultants.com
www.totalimageconsultants.com
617-625-5225 (office)
617-872-4791 (cell)

KATHARINE AND ALAN CAHN

Katharine Cahn, MSW, PhD
Executive Director
Center for the Improvement of Child and Family Services
Portland State University School of Social Work
Portland, Oregon

Alan Cahn
Landmark Education
acahn@landmarkeducation.net
www.landmarkeducation.com
415-616-2400 x2500 (office)

WENDY CAPLAND AND CHRIS MICHAUD

Wendy Capland
Vision Quest Consulting
www.visionquestconsulting.com
Christopher Michaud
Acceptance Group Realty
www.acceptancegroup.com
978-697-8568 (cell)

PHILIP CASS AND LAURA WEISEL

Philip Cass
Columbus Medical Association and Foundation
431 E. Broad Street
Columbus, OH 43215
pcass@goodhealthcolumbus.org
www.goodhealthcolumbus.org
614-240-7420 (office)
614-595-5152 (cell)
Laura Weisel
The TLP Group
PO Box 21510
Columbus, OH 43221
dr.weisel@powerpath.com
www.powerpath.com
614-850-8677 (office)
614-595-4665 (cell)

ALINA AND RON CHAND

Alina O. Chand
Ronald H. Chand
Chand Associates, Incorporated
12 South Street
Paxton, MA 01612
achand@charter.net
rchand@charter.net
508-735-9876 (cell - Alina)
508-868-9691 (cell - Ron)

JENNIFER CHRISTIAN AND DAVID SIKTBERG

Jennifer H. Christian, MD, MPH
David Siktberg
Webility Corporation
95 Woodridge Road
Wayland, MA 01778
jennifer.christian@webility.md
david.siktberg@webility.md
www.webility.md
508-358-5218 (office)
617-803-9835 (cell - Jennifer)
508-397-1204 (cell - David)

JEFFREY AND SANDY DAVIS

Jeffrey Davis
Mage LLC
119 Braintree Street, Suite 505
Boston MA 02134
JDavis@Mageusa.com
www.mageusa.com
JDavis25@Babson.edu
www.radioentrepreneurs.com
617-244-8366 (office)
617-462-4738 (cell)
Sandra Davis
HRG Development, Inc.
sandy.HRGDEV@comcast.net
617-775-5141 (cell)

ALLEN AND THERESA DAYTNER

Allen Daytner
Theresa Alfaro Daytner
Daytner Construction Group
114 S. Main Street, Suite 202
Mount Airy, MD 21771
add@daytnercorp.com
tad@daytnercorp.com
www.daytnercorp.com
301-829-1772 (office)

ANNE AND CHRISTOPHER ELLINGER

Anne Ellinger
Christopher Ellinger
True Story Theater
Arts Rising
Bolder Giving
Anne@TrueStoryTheater.org
www.TrueStoryTheater.org
Christopher@ArtsRising.net
www.ArtsRising.net
Jason Franklin, Executive Director
Bolder Giving
330 West 38th Street, Suite 505
New York, NY 10018
info@BolderGiving.org
www.BolderGiving.org
646-678-4394 (office)

MATTHEW AND TERCES ENGELHART

Matthew Engelhart
Terces Engelhart
Cafe Gratitude and Eternal Presence
160 14th Street
San Francisco, CA 94103
Marta Macbeth
marta@cafegratitude.com
www.cafegratitude.com
415-501-9678 (office)

CLAUDETTE AND ADE FAISON

Claudette C. Faison
Ade W. Faison
NY Youth At Risk
25 West 36th Street, 8th Floor
New York, NY 10018
Prudence Walters
prudence@nyyouthatrisk.org
www.nyyouthatrisk.org
212-791-4927 (office)

LAURIE AND JEFFREY FORD

Laurie Ford
3101 Splitrock Road
Columbus, OH 43221

laurie@laurieford.com
www.laurieford.com
614-921-8700 (office)
614-563-2530 (cell)
Jeffrey Ford
Fisher College of Business
The Ohio State University
750 Fisher Hall, 2100 Neil Avenue
Columbus, OH 43210
Ford.1@osu.edu
www.usingthefourconversations.com
www.professorford.com
614-921-8700 (office)
614-563-2095 (cell)

BARRY FRIEDMAN AND VALERIE GATES
Barry Friedman
Valerie Gates
Gates Studio
Integrated Branding Design
valerie@gatestudio.com
www.gatestudio.com
781-235-3480 (office)

SUZANNE AND DWIGHT FRINDT
Suzanne Mayo Frindt
Dwight Frindt
Northwest Office
2130 Partners, LLC
4580 Klahanie Drive, SE #503
Issaquah, WA 98029
Southern California Office
2130 Partners, LLC
PO Box 2366
Capistrano Beach, CA 92624
suzanne.frindt@2130partners.com
dwight.frindt@2130partners.com
www.2130partners.com
Northwest
425-427-2130 (office)
425-427-2130 (cell)
Southern California
949-489-2130 (office)
949-903-2130 (cell)

SANDY AND LON GOLNICK

Sandy Golnick
Lon Golnick
Relationship & Families ByDesign
7306 El Fuerte Street
Carlsbad, CA 92009
sandy@familiesbydesign.com
lon@familiesbydesign.com
www.familiesbydesign.com
www.relationshipbydesign.com
760-603-8343 (office)
760-702-1666 (cell - Sandy)
760-485-1026 (cell - Lon)

PETER HANSEN AND PETRA KRAULEDAT

Peter Hansen
Petra Krauledat
phansen5488@gmail.com
petrakrauledat@gmail.com

PETER KEVORKIAN AND PATTI GIULIANO

Dr. Peter Kevorkian
Dr. Patti Giuliano
Westwood Family Chiropractic
1446 High Street
Westwood, MA 02090
westwoodfamilychiropractic@gmail.com
www.westwoodfamilychiropractic.com
781-769-2500 (office)
339-225-0540 (cell - Peter)

GINA LAROCHE AND ALAN PRICE

Gina LaRoche
Seven Stones Leadership Group
275 West Rock Avenue
New Haven, CT 06515
gina@sevenstonesleadership.com
www.sevenstonesleadership.com
203-389-7645 (office)
Alan Price
Northeast Utilities
107 Selden Street
Berlin, CT 06037

alan@readytolead.net
www.readytolead.net

JEAN AND HOWARD LE VAUX

Jean Le Vaux
Howard A. Le Vaux
Le Vaux Associates (Coldwell Banker)
171 Huron Avenue
Cambridge, MA 02138
jeanlevaux@gmail.com
levaux@gmail.com
www.newenglandmoves.com
617-844-2743 (office - Jean)
617-844-2742 (office - Howard)
617-460-0436 (cell - Jean)
617-460-6851 (cell - Howard)

KATY AND PHILIP LEAKEY

Katy Leakey
Philip Leakey
The Leakey Collection
thebush@leakeycollection.com
www.leakeycollection.com
www.zulugrass.com

JESSICA LIPNACK AND JEFFREY STAMPS

Jessica Lipnack
NetAge, Inc.
PO Box 650037
West Newton, MA 02465
jessica.lipnack@netage.com
www.netage.com
617-965-3340 (office)
617-510-7290 (cell)

NICK AND MITRA LORE

Nick Lore
Mitra Mortazavi Lore
Rockport Institute
10124 Lakewood Drive
Rockville, MD 20850
info@rockportinstitute.com
www.rockportinstitute.com
301-340-6600 (office)

SHERRI AND TERRY MCARDLE

Sherri McArdle
Terry McArdle
The McArdle Ramerman Center
693 East Avenue
Rochester, NY 14607
SherriM@leadershiprising.com
Terry.McArdle@gmail.com
www.LeadershipRising.com
585-325-1210 (office)

DAVID NICHOLAS AND DAVID MIRANOWICZ

David Nicholas
David Miranowicz
David Nicholas International, Inc.
info@makeupdni.com
www.makeupdni.com
617-242-0177 (office)

SCOTT AND SUE RICHARDSON

Scott Richardson
Sue Richardson
Longwood Software, Inc.
107 Main Street
Maynard, MA 01754
scott@longwoodsoftware.com
sue@longwoodsoftware.com
www.longwoodsoftware.com
www.revbase.com
www.forfile.com
978-897-2900 (office)
978-337-6957 (cell - Scott)

JUDY ROSENBERG AND ELIOT WINOGRAD

Judy Rosenberg
Eliot Winograd
Rosie's Bakery
9 Boylston Street
Chestnut Hill Shopping Center
Chestnut Hill, MA 02467
judyrosenberg@mac.com
ewinograd@rosiesbakery.com
www.rosiesbakery.com
857-255-2094 (office)

617-548-2730 (cell - Judy)
617-733-3073 (cell - Eliot)

STEVEN AND MARJORIE SAYER

Steven Sayer
Marjorie Sayer
1186 Melendy Hill Drive
Guilford, VT 05301
Equipsystem, Inc.
equipsys@aol.com
ssayer7@gmail.com
marjorie.sayer@gmail.com
802-254 1059 (office)

ELLYN SPRAGINS AND JOHN WITTY

Ellyn Spragins
What I Know Now Enterprises
John Witty
322 South Main Street
Pennington, NJ 08534
ellynspragins@gmail.com
www.letterstomyyoungerself.com
609-818-1429 (office)
609-731-2336 (cell)
jtwitman@aol.com
609-818-1458 (office)
609-731-2356 (cell)

DOROTHY AND WAYNE STINGLEY

Dorothy Stingley
Wayne Stingley
Stingley Management, Inc., DBA McDonald's
23224 N 95th Place
Scottsdale, AZ 85255
dsting1952@stingleymcd.com
480-585-4142 (office)

LYNNE AND BILL TWIST

Lynne Twist
Soul of Money Institute
#3 - 5th Avenue
San Francisco, CA 94118
lynne@soulofmoney.org
www.soulofmoney.org

415-386-5599 (office)
www.pachamama.org
Bill Twist
The Pachamama Alliance
1009 General Kennedy Avenue
San Francisco, CA 94129
btwist@pachamama.org
www.pachamama.org
415-561-4522 (office)

WYNN AND DOUGLAS WAGGONER

Wynn Waggoner
Wynn Interiors and Intuitive Design
Douglas Waggoner
The Art of Naturally Fallen Timber
7483 Flagstaff Road
Boulder, CO 80302
wynninteriors@wispertel.net
www.wynninteriors.com
naturallyfallentimber@wispertel.net
www.naturallyfallentimber.com
303-546-6199 (office)

JOYCE AND JACK ZIMMERMAN

Joyce Zimmerman
Jack Zimmerman
joyciezimmerman@gmail.com
jackzim25@gmail.com

BIBLIOGRAPHY

Beattie, Melodie. *The Language of Letting Go: Hazelton Meditation Series.* Center City, MN: Hazelton Publishing, 1990.

Benson, Robert. *Between the Dreaming and the Coming True: The Road Home to God.* San Francisco: HarperSanFrancisco, 1996.

Block, Peter. *Community: The Structure of Belonging.* San Francisco, CA: Berrett-Koehler Publishers, Inc., 2009.

Boorstein, Sylvia. *Happiness Is an Inside Job: Practicing for a Joyful Life.* New York: Random House, 2008.

_____ *Don't Just Do Something, Sit There: A Mindfulness Retreat with Sylvia Boorstein.* New York: Harper Collins Publishing, 1996.

Brady, Mark. *The Wisdom of Listening.* Somerville, MA: Wisdom Publications, 2005.

Chodron, Pema. *Comfortable with Uncertainty: 108 Teachings on Cultivating Fearlessness and Compassion.* Boston, MA: Shambhala, 2003.

Coontz, Stephanie. *Marriage, a History: How Love Conquered Marriage.* New York: Penguin Books, 2006.

Covey, Stephen M.R. and Rebecca R. Merrill. *The Speed of Trust: The One Thing that Changes Everything.* New York: Simon and Schuster, 2006.

Dyer, Wayne. *The Power of Intention.* Carlsbad, CA: Hay House, 2005.

Ferrari, Bernard T. *Power Listening: Mastering the Most Critical Business Skill of All.* New York: Penguin Group, 2012.

Gottman, John. *Why Marriages Succeed or Fail: And How You Can Make Yours Last.* London, UK: Bloomsbury Publishing, 1995

Hanh, Thich Nhat. *The Miracle of Mindfulness: An Introduction to the Practice of Meditation.* Boston, MA: Beacon Press, 1999.

_____ *True Love: A Practice for Awakening the Heart.* Boston, MA: Shambhala, 2011.

_____ *Anger: Wisdom for Cooling the Flames.* New York: Riverhead Books, 2002.

Hawken, Paul. *Blessed Unrest: How the Largest Social Movement in History is Restoring Grace, Justice and Beauty to the World.* San Diego, CA: Baker and Taylor, 2008.

Hoppe, Michael H. *Active Listening: Improve Your Ability to Listen and Lead.* Greensboro, NC: Center for Creative Leadership, 2007.

Hyde, Lewis: *The Gift: Imagination and the Erotic Life of Property.* New York, NY: Vintage, 1979.

Jones, Van. *Rebuild the Dream.* New York: Nation Books, 2012.

Kahane, Adam. *Power and Love: A Theory and Practice of Social Change.* San Francisco, CA: Berrett-Koehler Publishers, Inc. 2010.

Marshack PhD, Kathy J. *Entrepreneurial Couples: Making it Work at Work and at Home.* Palo Alto, CA: Davies-Black Publisher, 1998.

Mipham, Sakong and Pema Chodron. *Turning the Mind Into An Ally.* Boston, MA: Shambhala, 2004.

Mipham, Sakong. *Running with the Mind of Meditation: Lessons for Training Body and Mind.* Boston, MA: Shambhala, 2012.

Schlesinger, Leonard A. and Charles F. Kiefer. *Just Start.* Boston, MA: Harvard Business Review Press, 2012.

Schwarmer, Otto. *Theory U: Leading from the Future as it Emerges.* San Francisco, CA: Berrett-Koehler Publishers, Inc., 2007.

Senge, Peter. *The Fifth Discipline: The Art & Practice of the Learning Organization.* New York: Doubleday, 2006.

Stone, Douglas, Bruce Patton, Sheila Heen & Roger Fisher. *Difficult Conversations: How to Discuss What Matters Most.* New York: Penguin Books, 2010

Trungpa, Chogyam, Carolyn Rose Gimian and Pema Chodron. *Smile at Fear: Awakening the True Heart of Bravery.* Boston, MA: Shambhala, 2010.

Trungpa, Chogyam, Carolyn Rose Gimian & Sherub Chodzin Kohn. *Work, Sex, Money: Real Life on the Path of Mindfulness.* Boston, MA: Shambhala, 2011.

Twist, Lynne and Teresa Barker. *The Soul of Money: Reclaiming the Wealth of Our Inner Resources.* New York: WW Norton & Company, 2006

Ulrich, David, Wendy Ulrich and Marshall Goldsmith. *The Why of Work: How Great Leaders Build Abundant Organizations That Win.* New York: McGraw-Hill, 2010.

Watzlawick, Paul. *Change: Principles of Problem Formation and Problem Resolution.* New York: WW Norton & Company, 2011.

Zaffron, Steve and Dave Logan. *The Three Laws of Performance: Rewriting the Future of Your Organization and Your Life*. San Francisco, CA: Jossey-Bass, 2009.

Zander, Rosemund Stone and Benjamin Zander. *The Art of Possibility: Transforming Professional and Personal life*. Boston, MA: Harvard Business School Press, 2000.

14149107R00098

Made in the USA
Charleston, SC
24 August 2012